English Period Furniture

English Period Furniture

Charles H. Hayward

Evans Brothers Limited London

Published by Evans Brothers Limited
Montague House, Russell Square
London WC1

© Evans Brothers Limited 1959
First published 1936

Sixteenth printing, revised and reset
© Evans Brothers Limited 1977

420297502

Set in 11 on 12 point Baskerville
Printed in Great Britain by
The Whitefriars Press Ltd,
London and Tonbridge

ISBN 0 237 44867 X   PRA 5396

Contents

By the same author

To My Wife
without whose forbearance this
book would never have been completed

Mahogany secretaire-bookcase. Specially interesting are the curved cornice (which would require that the side return mouldings would be of different section from that of the curved front), and the beautifully proportioned tracery of the doors. Note, too, the curved French feet. Late 18th century. Photograph by courtesy of Collins Antiques, Wheathampstead.

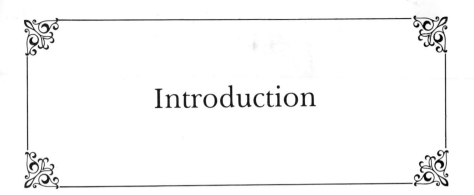

Introduction

In writing this book I have endeavoured to show the kind of furniture in common use in England from about 1500 up to the middle years of the Victorian period. It is an extraordinarily interesting subject, one which goes far beyond a mere recitation of styles. It tells of the lives people led and the conditions they had to face, the whole linked up with the historical events that went to the evolution of Britain as we know it today.

The fact is that the furniture made at any particular period was largely the result of the circumstances of life at that time, particularly in the early years. Later when choice was largely dictated by fashion rather than by necessity there was not the same strong reflection of life in general, because when people do things merely because other people do them the result has less meaning than when cicumstances force a line of action upon them.

To give added interest I have included a short section on French furniture from about 1643 to the close of the eighteenth century. This is nothing more than a brief description, but it is useful to have a general idea of the type of furniture being made in France because it has at various times had a strong influence on things made in Britain. The plates of measured drawings too should be of value in that they show proportions, details of mouldings, thicknesses of parts, and so on. In the same way the analysis of chairs is an essentially practical chapter in which I have tried to show the problems of the chair-maker.

I have a theory that practical considerations have always had a stronger influence on design than is generally realized, and I hope that this will become obvious to the reader. It is a subject that I have developed more fully in my book, *Antique or Fake?*

In conclusion I should like to thank those who have been kind enough to give me permission to take down details of old furniture in their possession, or to provide photographs of it for this new edition.

C. H. Hayward
St. Albans, 1977.

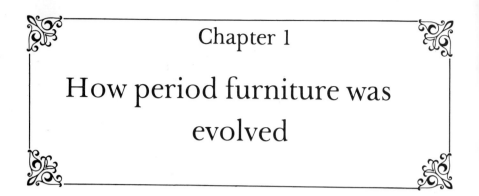

Chapter 1

How period furniture was evolved

The person who takes up the study of antique furniture for the first time may well ask why it was that bygone days produced a definite kind of furniture apparently peculiar to the particular period when it was made. Why did it have these characteristic features? Such points as the use of local timber, or the crudeness of workmanship due to primitive tools, may be obvious, but neither of these can account for *all* the features of a period piece, nor explain why the productions of one age were different from those of another.

Perhaps the simplest way of approaching the subject is to consider what is happening today, and see whether the conditions with which we are now familiar are moulding a style which future generations will be able to recognize. Is there now a twentieth century style in furniture just as there was in, say, the mid-eighteenth century? We see in the shops and in books items labelled 'up-to-date', 'modern', and so on, but do those terms really denote an established style which can be said to be characteristic of this age?

In a limited sense the present period has certain features which belong to it, and these in their combination presumably do form a style. Chief among them are the recessed plinths and tops, almost complete absence of carving except on reproduction work, the restricted use of the framed and panelled door and its replacement by wide flat doors covered by finely-figured veneers, and the use of plain, square fillets in place of the more or less elaborate mouldings of a few years back.

Now many of these features are the result of conditions or circumstances which are peculiar to the present time. For instance, the manufacture of reliable plywood in thick panels and the production of laminated board and chipboard has made it possible to do away largely with the older framed-up construction in which the panel was free to shrink in grooves. Good manufactured board will neither shrink nor warp, and in its nature it can be obtained in extremely wide boards. Thus we have the wide doors and panels which are so essentially a part of modern design.

At the same time, plywood is made in an inexpensive wood which is

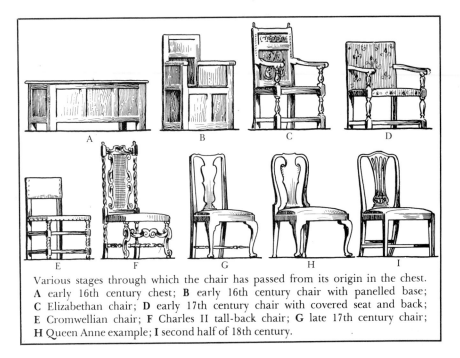

Various stages through which the chair has passed from its origin in the chest.
A early 16th century chest; **B** early 16th century chair with panelled base;
C Elizabethan chair; **D** early 17th century chair with covered seat and back;
E Cromwellian chair; **F** Charles II tall-back chair; **G** late 17th century chair;
H Queen Anne example; **I** second half of 18th century.

remarkable more for its reliability than for the beauty of its grain. In any case, the layers are usually 'rotary cut,' which means that they are sliced from the log circumferentially, and this produces a very wild, uninteresting grain. Hence, veneering is a necessity, and so comes the widespread use of veneers today.

Another factor which has caused veneer to be widely used is the comparative scarcity of finely figured-woods. It is difficult to obtain a really fine solid board of mahogany or walnut today. The scarcity has made it so valuable that it is cut up almost entirely for veneers. Oak is perhaps the only wood in which the rarity is not so noticeable, and even here it is used widely in veneer form for laying on plywood. This scarcity will undoubtedly be more marked during the years to come, so that one is justified in predicting that veneer will be used even more in the future.

The absence of carving today is largely due to economic circumstances. Carving is an expensive process, and since the world slump, beginning in 1929, it has never recovered its popularity; usually it appears only on reproductions. To obtain a decorative effect with veneers in various built-up patterns is cheaper.

Thus there certainly are features which are typical of the times in modern furniture. However, one cannot pretend that the characteristics are so marked as in the periods of the past. The truth is that there are so many things from which to choose and so many easy ways of doing them that, so far as design is concerned, furniture is remarkable more for its variety than for its following of any general style. One has only to walk through a large furniture store to see the truth of this. You can buy a

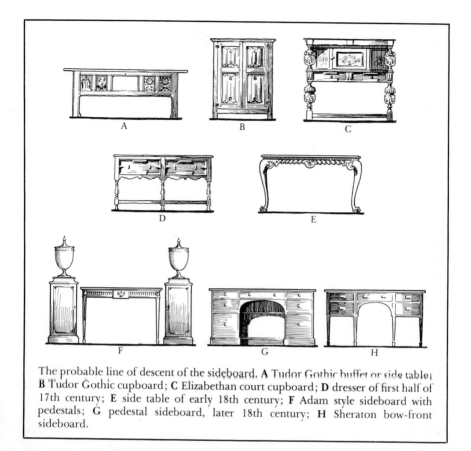

The probable line of descent of the sideboard. **A** Tudor Gothic buffet or side table; **B** Tudor Gothic cupboard; **C** Elizabethan court cupboard; **D** dresser of first half of 17th century; **E** side table of early 18th century; **F** Adam style sideboard with pedestals; **G** pedestal sideboard, later 18th century; **H** Sheraton bow-front sideboard.

sideboard in any wood from walnut to thuya, and it can be in any style from the Spanish Gothic to the latest creation in Macassar ebony.

A realization of these facts is of tremendous help in appreciating why period furniture came into existence in the form it did; it makes clear why a knowledge of the conditions and circumstances of past times is so helpful in dating a piece. Except for the few points noted, modern furniture is under the influence almost entirely of fashion. As one goes backward in history fashion plays less and less a part in style. Fashion is usually possible only to people who have reached a certain degree of affluence, and the farther back one goes the less there was to spare for anything beyond what was absolutely necessary. When a man spends a day tracking down an animal in order to provide for the next meal, it is hardly to be expected that his thoughts will extend to the fine arts.

So with the story of furniture. When bare necessity is the only guiding principle there is little room for the luxury of fashion. When you have only one wood to use, a very limited kit of tools, and only human arms to do everything from cutting down the tree to carving the cabinet, or whatever it may be, there is not a great deal of room for varying the style.

From all this it becomes plain that the circumstances at any particular period necessarily have their effects on the woodwork being produced. The intermarriage of a king with the royal house of a foreign country may cause a foreign influence to creep in owing to the migration of craftsmen from abroad. A voyage of discovery may result in the introduction of a new wood, or the imposition of a tax may cause its importation almost to cease. Fashion in dress, too, exerted an influence on furniture. And finally there is the craftsmen's skill at any given time.

To sum up the influences which result in the production of the particular kind of furniture of a certain period, there are:

General circumstances Whether, for instance, men were able to afford more than just necessities; transport facilities; whether conditions were peaceful or not; and so on.

Housing conditions Whether people had separate dwelling-houses or lived in grouped communities, of which the central feature was the great hall of a country mansion.

Historical events The Reformation, for example, which resulted in the suppression of the monasteries and the consequent decline of ecclesiastical influence.

Material available Tropical woods such as mahogany and satinwood obviously could not be used until voyages of discovery enabled such woods to be imported.

Skill of workers Fine cabinet work, as distinct from joinery, was unknown until towards the end of the seventeenth century when a new technique was evolved.

Individual influences Before the first half of the eighteenth century not a single name stands out as an influence on furniture design.

Peculiarities of locality These are mainly peculiarities which are handed down by a trade convention. It is not always clear why certain districts had their own ways of making one or another item of furniture, but it is an undoubted fact that these peculiarities did exist.

Outside influences The Renaissance is an example of a huge influence which affected every country in Europe.

From the foregoing it might appear that at a given period one sort of furniture was made to the exclusion of every other kind. In a general sense this was so, but a certain overlapping in style was inevitable. The lack of easy transport often resulted in a district being more or less cut off from the outside world. A man might spend his life without travelling more than a short distance from home. As a consequence ideas were

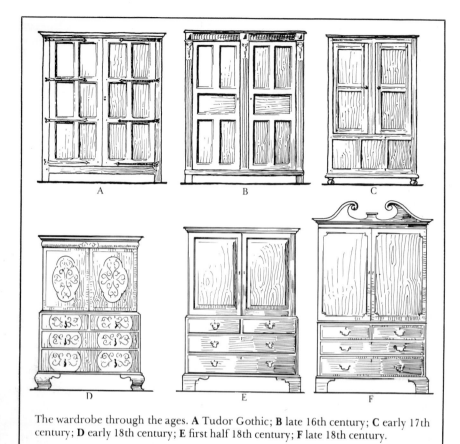

The wardrobe through the ages. **A** Tudor Gothic; **B** late 16th century; **C** early 17th century; **D** early 18th century; **E** first half 18th century; **F** late 18th century.

liable to cling longer than might be imagined. A new influence might begin in London owing to, say, the settling of foreign craftsmen, but it would probably be many years before such influence would reach a town some fifty or a hundred miles away. A traveller passing through might speak of it in an inn, but it would convey little to a carpenter listening to the conversation. It would not be until somebody living in the district bought a piece of furniture in the new style in London and had it carried down to his home that the local craftsmen, by actually seeing it, could imitate the style. Even then, with no previous experience, they would probably make but a poor job of it.

Then, again, take the case of the introduction of a new wood, say, mahogany. It was expensive enough to transport from abroad, and, if to that the cost of carrying it far into the country had to be added, it would raise the cost of the furniture tremendously. Remember that the condition of the roads (where they existed at all) was simply appalling. Thus it is often found that oak was used in country districts during periods when mahogany was used exclusively in London and the large towns. Take, for instance, the vast number of oak grandfather clock cases one finds in shops. These were invariably made during the eighteenth century, at a time when nothing but mahogany, satinwood, and other tropical woods were used in the towns. They were made in oak either because it was the only wood available in the country district, or because it was considerably cheaper.

Quite apart from this there is always the question of individual taste. Fashion might decree that a certain wood should be used or a certain style followed. The majority would follow it, but some craftsmen, either unable to adapt their ideas or unwilling to do so, would continue on the old lines. Or it might be that a man had retained the old furniture of his grandfather's time, and, requiring a new piece, would have it made to match it. Another point to bear in mind is that many pieces of eighteenth century style were made in Victorian times, and their recognition calls for considerable experience.

Thus it happens that there is constant overlapping in the periods, and it is impossible to lay down an invariable rule. It is true that there are certain dates and facts which form a definite guide. As an example, mahogany was first imported into this country by Sir Walter Raleigh in the late sixteenth century, but it was not in anything like general use until after 1725. Consequently an English piece of furniture in mahogany could not possibly be earlier than the former date, and is unlikely to be earlier than the second. Apart from this, however, one has to be prepared to allow considerable latitude. All one can do is to indicate what was the general custom of a period and so follow the main chain of evolution.

Readers who wish to carry their study of the subject farther are advised to turn their attention to old furniture itself, for it is only by being in actual contact with it that one comes to recognize it. One word of warning is that the world today is filled with fakes and reproductions which may give an impression that is wholly erroneous. So long as antique furniture is popular – and consequently fetches a good price – so will the faker flourish. Were he to cease his activities tomorrow, there are enough spurious pieces in the world to make the expert spend most of his time, not in saying to what period a piece belongs, but in deciding whether it is genuine or not. It is a problem now; what it will be like in fifty and more years' time when all the present-day innocent reproductions have had time to mellow, scarcely bears thinking about.

However, our museums contain many specimens of undoubted authenticity which the reader should study, and attention is also drawn to the many genuine old pieces, mostly of oak, to be found in churches all over Britain. Mansions, too, have their quota of antique pieces and the reader, in addition to noting the material, design, construction, and so on (aspects which this book endeavours to cover), should note carefully the *surface*. It is a thing that cannot be described or photographed accurately. It is an indescribable 'something' recognition of which one acquires only with long practice, and the only way to learn is to study authentic specimens. It is perhaps the one thing that the faker cannot imitate, though he may get over the difficulty in another way.

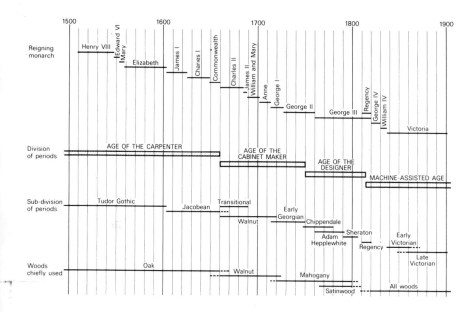

In the meantime this book shows the kind of furniture that men made years ago, the way they made it, and the detail they cut into it, and this will go far in enabling the layman to recognize old furniture, or the craftsman to reproduce it.

British Monarchs

Henry VII, 1485–1509
Henry VIII, 1509–1547
Edward VI, 1547–1553
Mary, 1553–1558
Elizabeth, 1558–1603
James I, 1603–1625
Charles I, 1625–1649
(Commonwealth, 1649–1660)
Charles II, 1660–1685
James II, 1685–1688

William and Mary, 1689–1702
Anne, 1702–1714
George I, 1714–1727
George II, 1727–1760
George III, 1760–1820
(Regency, 1810–1820)
George IV, 1820–1830
William IV, 1830–1837
Victoria, 1837–1901

French Monarchs

Francis I, 1515–1547
Henry II, 1547–1559
Francis II, 1559–1560
Charles IX, 1560–1574
Henry III, 1574–1589
Henry IV, 1589–1610
Louis XIII, 1610–1643
Louis XIV, 1643–1715

Louis XV, 1715–1774
Louis XVI, 1774–1793
Directory, 1795–1799
Consulate, 1799–1804
Empire (Napoleon I), 1804–1814
Louis XVIII, 1814–1822
Charles X, 1822–1830
Louis Philippe, 1830–1848

There are many terms which serve to denote the period to which a piece of furniture may belong. Most of them are taken from the names of reigning monarchs, but for the purpose of this book the three to four hundred years beginning in 1500 are divided into parts, each of which forms a natural group in itself.

They are useful titles because each suggests a characteristic peculiar to the furniture of the time. In early days the carpenter tackled almost every kind of job in woodwork. The furniture he made was incidental, and the construction and treatment therefore bore the stamp of a craftsman used to large joinery work. Hence it is termed the age of the carpenter.

After the Restoration in 1660 it became customary for certain woodworkers to specialize in furniture-making only, and as a consequence an entirely new technique peculiar to furniture came into being. It was the age of the cabinet maker.

About the middle of the eighteenth century certain schools of design were formed, and architects like Adam came to design furniture specially for the houses they built. As a result most of the cabinet makers began to follow one or other of these sources of inspiration, so that the furniture had individual characteristics instead of following a more general fashion. It is thus called the age of the designer.

Lastly there is the period from about 1820 when machines began to be used. At first they were of the simplest type used mostly for the conversion of timber, but becoming more sophisticated and used for many other purposes such as planing and moulding. At the same time they seldom replaced handwork entirely so that one frequently finds both hand and machine work in the same job.

For convenience each of these groups is subdivided as shown below.

The Age of the Carpenter, 1500–1660	Tudor Gothic	1500–1603
	Jacobean	1603–1660
The Age of the Cabinet-maker, 1660–1750	Transitional	1660–1690
	Walnut	1660–1720
	Early Georgian	1714–1750
The Age of the Designer, 1750–1800	Chippendale	1745–1780
	Adam	1760–1792
	Hepplewhite	1760–1790
	Sheraton	1790–1806
	Regency and George IV	1810–1830
Machine-assisted Age 1820 onwards	Victorian	1837–

The above dates are approximate only, and are intended to indicate the years when furniture of a certain style was mainly produced. They do not necessarily show the year in which any of the designers or cabinet makers died.

The Great Hall, Penshurst Place, Kent. In these early days there was none of the privacy which a country family enjoys to-day. The whole household from the owner of the mansion to the lowest retainer dined together in the great hall. Two of the great tables used for the purpose are shown above. Apart from these and a number of stools and forms, and possibly one chair for the chief diner, there would probably be no other furniture. 14th century.

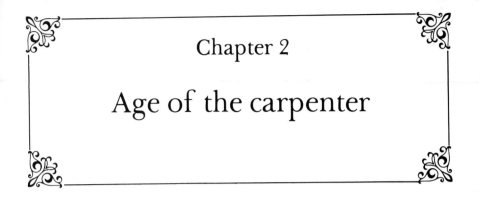

Chapter 2

Age of the carpenter

Tudor Gothic period

So few examples of English domestic furniture dating from a period earlier than the accession of Henry VIII exist, that for the purpose of this book there is little to be gained from going back earlier than the end of the fifteenth century, except to see how what had gone before influenced the woodwork that was to come. The longer the period that elapses, the greater the chances of destruction and decay, and the troublous times through which this country went in the Middle Ages certainly enabled destruction to carry out its work of waste. An army marching through an enemy country would spare little that came its way, and even in peaceful times the outbreak of fire must have been an ever-present source of danger. Domestic houses were invariably built of timber and, as the fire on the open hearth was never or seldom allowed to go out, being just fanned to a flame every morning, the chances of the building catching fire must have been high.

Apart from this, however, furniture was a rare commodity in those days. Even in the larger houses the hall would contain little more than a large table, a chair for the owner of the house, forms and stools for the rest of the household, a cupboard of some sort, and a chest. In the chief sleeping room there would be a bed, a chest to hold clothes, and possibly a cupboard or press. The sleeping rooms for the less important people might contain little more than a mattress or even just a couch of rushes. Smaller houses were furnished on a correspondingly smaller scale, so that it becomes clear that the chances of survival were extremely small.

The closing years of the fifteenth century mark the beginning of a change in conditions. The accession of Henry VII had brought to an end the long period of strife known as the Wars of the Roses, and with the feeling of comparative security people began to find time to turn their attention to their houses. There could have been but little encouragement for a man to beautify his house when he knew that it might be burnt over his head either by the first party of soldiers that came marching through, or by a band of insurgents such as that headed by Jack Cade.

Fig. 1 Two chests showing the two systems of construction. The chest above consists of a series of boards nailed together, and is very elementary. It is inevitable that the wide front and back will split owing to shrinkage, since they are held rigidly to the sides the grain of which is upright. Early 16th century. This difficulty is overcome in the framed-up chest below, in which the panels are free to shrink in their grooves. Second half 16th century.

His first thought would have been to fortify it against attack. It was not until warfare came to an end that he felt justified in making, or was able to make, himself more comfortable. Not that the change came quickly. The wars had bled the country of its manhood so that many a man who might have spent his life peaceably in making useful things was pressed into the service of his local lord to fight on whichever side happened to be in favour locally.

Coming of the Renaissance Nevertheless the coming of peace did encourage the development of the home as distinct from the fortified house and, what was equally important, it set the stage for the remarkable influence of the Renaissance, which was to sweep across the country during the sixteenth century. It is an extraordinary thing that people can be carried off their feet, so to speak, by an intangible thing like this Renaissance. It is hard to find a name by which to call it. It was just a great influence which was to leave its mark on all the arts and crafts, and alter even the very lives of people.

To understand it fully one must realize that hitherto the crafts had been dominated entirely by the Gothic. People knew no other style. In architecture it had developed from the Norman at the end of the twelfth century, and had become almost a creed, the absolutism of which it was heresy to doubt. It was in fact closely bound up with the church, which had been the seat of learning and the consequent fountain-head of ideas and knowledge ever since the coming of the Normans. Every monastery had its group of stonemasons, carpenters, carvers, and so on.

The carpenters engaged on secular work had only one source from which to draw their ideas, the church, and a man called upon to make, say, a chest simply copied whatever detail he might find in a building, often with the most delightful disregard for its true meaning. Thus one often finds details used in woodwork which belong entirely to the technique of stone masonry.

The point I wish to make clear is that until the coming of the Renaissance all the woodwork was entirely Gothic in detail, form, and construction and as a consequence, when new ideas began to filter through, people did not know quite what to make of them, and they became little more than a grafting of Renaissance detail to a groundwork of Gothic. This will become more obvious when we come to examine individual pieces.

It was a condition that was aggravated by the fact that the early workers did not understand the spirit of the Renaissance. They regarded the details as just so many *motifs* to be used in any convenient way that suggested itself, and the result was often a curious mixture. It must be remembered that the Renaissance filtered through from abroad. It was entirely new. It was not like the Gothic, which was a natural development on lines which were built up on experience. It will be recognized by the use of the Roman orders of architecture, often wrongly applied, the intricately interwoven strapwork, carved egg-and-tongue mouldings, and all the many other details that had belonged to Rome in its glory.

Evolution of the chest

We have spoken of the chest as being part of the furnishing of the early house, and we deal with it first, not only because it was a most important piece of furniture, but because so many other pieces were evolved from it. It was used for all sorts of purposes: the storing of clothes or valuables, for a travelling chest, as a seat, or (in the larger sizes) even as a bed. In fact it was its all-round usefulness that was its great virtue, and accounts for the comparatively large numbers which have survived.

Early hollowed-out chests   In its earliest form it was merely hollowed out of a solid baulk of timber, the lid usually following the line of the trunk in shape and so being rounded. Such chests belong generally to a period before the fourteenth century, after which the more economical method of jointing up timber was evolved. Fig. 2 is an example.

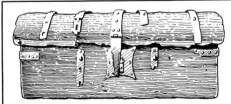

Fig. 2 Old chest in church at Harbledown. The lid is hollowed out of a solid baulk of timber, the curve approximating to that of the tree trunk from which it was cut. Probably 13th century.

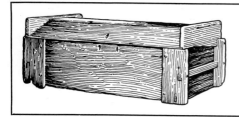

Fig. 3 Chest with pin-hinged lid. Although probably made in the 15th century, the construction is typical of an earlier period. All the wood is cleft and finished with the adze.

A curious example of how convention sets its stamp on things is shown in the next example, Fig. 3, which exemplifies the next stage in which separate boards were pegged together. Note how the lid, although not actually rounded, is raised in the centre and so is a survival of the older hollowed-out solid lid. Another feature of special interest is the way it is hinged. The end pieces into which the lid boards are housed are made extra wide at the back and fit outside the ends of the lower chest portion. Pegs passing through both enable the lid to be raised. It was a system of hingeing (usually termed pin hingeing) which survived until some time during the thirteenth century, when it was replaced by the more convenient metal strap hinges.

Planked chests   At the time our story begins – the late fifteenth century – most chests were little more than a series of four boards nailed or pegged together to form the sides, and a bottom and lid. It was a method of construction about which there was something rather obvious. It was essentially simple, a serious consideration in days when every operation had to be done entirely by hand, and up to a point it served its purpose.

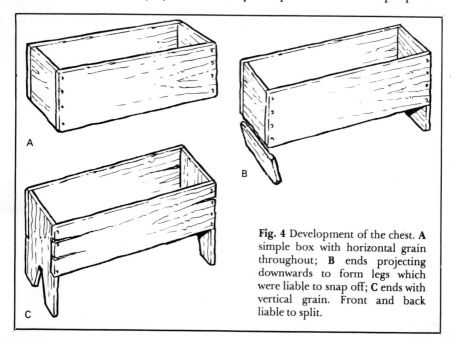

Fig. 4 Development of the chest. **A** simple box with horizontal grain throughout; **B** ends projecting downwards to form legs which were liable to snap off; **C** ends with vertical grain. Front and back liable to split.

It must have occurred to people quite early on, however, that it was desirable to raise the chest bottom up from the floor, and so came the idea of extending the ends downwards to form a sort of trestle end as at Fig. 4B. This, of course, necessitated having the grain of the ends vertical rather than horizontal otherwise they would be liable to snap off. In solving one problem, however, they created another. Since wood is liable to shrink across the grain as it dries (never along the length) the vertical grain of the ends neccessarily resisted the shrinkage of the front and back, and consequently splits and cracks were liable to develop as at Fig. 4C. It is this that accounts for the bad condition in which the fronts and backs of these planked chests are often found. Fig. 5 and 6 are examples of the type.

Framed-up construction   It was to overcome this fundamental fault that the panelled system of construction was evolved, in which the strength was provided by a framework joined at the corners with mortise and

Fig. 5   Fig. 7

Fig. 5 (left) Planked chest with carved front. This exemplifies the early, simple construction in which the front and back are merely nailed to the sides. The carving is purely Gothic in character. Early 16th century.

Fig. 7 Framed-up chest with linenfold panels. Here the panels are held in the grooves of a framework and so are free to shrink without danger of their splitting. Compare with chest, **Fig. 5**. Early 16th century.

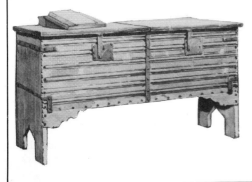

Fig. 6 Another chest of the planked type. This is at the church of Great Canfield, Essex and is remarkable in that it is of pine rather than of oak. Front and back board are 32 mm. (1$\frac{3}{16}$ in.) thick.

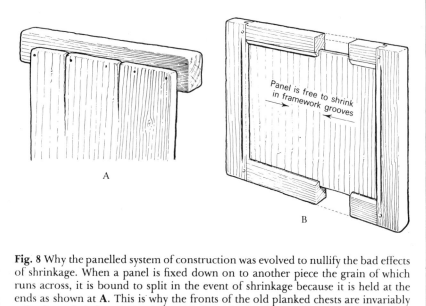

Fig. 8 Why the panelled system of construction was evolved to nullify the bad effects of shrinkage. When a panel is fixed down on to another piece the grain of which runs across, it is bound to split in the event of shrinkage because it is held at the ends as shown at **A**. This is why the fronts of the old planked chests are invariably split along their length. In the panelled method **B** the panel is held loosely in the grooves and can so shrink without danger of splitting. The top and bottom rails provide the necessary strength across the grain.

tenon joints, the centre portion being filled in with a panel which rested in grooves worked in the inner edges of the framework. The panel was entirely free in the grooves, so that in the event of shrinkage no harm whatever would be done. Fig. 8 is a comparison between the two methods of construction.

The effect of this new form of construction on the chest is shown in Fig. 7. It is virtually four separate frames except that the legs are part of both front and sides. The bad effects of shrinkage are eliminated, since the panels are free to shrink.

Whilst still on this subject of panelling, it is instructive to note that the width of the individual panels was seldom more than that of a single board, this saving the necessity of jointing. It is a useful point to remember because it accounts for the comparatively narrow panels found in early oak work.

Treatment of panels

Linenfold panels A favourite method of embellishing the panels of these chests was to carve them in the linenfold pattern as in Fig. 7, and many ingenious theories have been put forward to account for the origin of this device. That it was carved to represent a piece of folded linen is

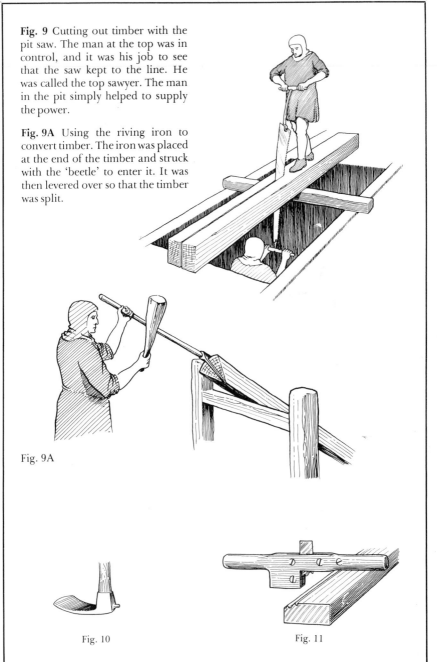

Fig. 9 Cutting out timber with the pit saw. The man at the top was in control, and it was his job to see that the saw kept to the line. He was called the top sawyer. The man in the pit simply helped to supply the power.

Fig. 9A Using the riving iron to convert timber. The iron was placed at the end of the timber and struck with the 'beetle' to enter it. It was then levered over so that the timber was split.

Fig. 9A

Fig. 10

Fig. 11

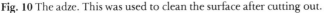

Fig. 10 The adze. This was used to clean the surface after cutting out.

Fig. 11 Scratch tool. The chief purpose of this was to work mouldings. It was simply worked back and forth.

Fig. 12 Examples of Tudor Gothic panels. **A, B** Gothic panels with opening pierced right through; **C** Linenfold panel; **D** Curved rib design; All early 16th century. Tudor Gothic panels with Renaissance influence; **E** Renaissance motif; mid. 16th century; **F** Romayne panel, about 1530.

undoubtedly true, but it probably owed its origin to a practical reason, especially as the earlier patterns were of simple form, just an ogee-shaped section, thin at the edges and rising to a point at the centre.

Most early oak was riven, that is, the log was cleft at the end with a wedge and so forced apart. The method was far less laborious than sawing, and it was stronger since it followed the natural line of cleavage. Fig. 9A shows the process. At the same time the boards were not so straight and the surface was liable to have ridges in it. These ridges may have suggested the lines of the folded linen, and in any case the edges had to be reduced in thickness to enable them to fit in the grooves of the framing. Thus it seems to be a case of the craftsmen making the most of the peculiarities of the material, and adapting the design to suit the natural formation.

The enlarged illustration Fig. 12C shows a linenfold pattern in closer detail in which the wood is cut thin at the sides to enable it to enter the grooves. This cutting-away forms a part of the design. Note also that the recessing of the groundwork at top and bottom to throw the folds into relief answers the same purpose.

Curved rib panels Another form of decoration was what is usually termed the curved rib design, an example of which is also given at Fig. 12D. It probably owed its origin to the same causes as the linenfold. If the two illustrations Fig. 12C and D are compared it will be seen that the linenfold has the same downward curve in the ends of the folds at the top. The only fundamental difference is the introduction of the centre fold. The thinning of the edges occurs in both, and the riving of the timber would make it suitable for either one or the other in accordance with the amount of timber left by the cleavage. In fact it may be that the craftsman decided which treatment he would give after the timber had been riven. Or, alternatively, assuming that he had some timber already riven, he would select that which was the more suitable for the design he had in mind.

Tracery designs This, however, is largely theory, and we may now turn to yet another kind of panel, the origin of which is more certain. This is the traceried panel of which two examples are given at Fig. 12A and B. They were taken from the Gothic traceried windows which were a common feature of buildings of the period. Generally they were pierced right through, and this had the advantage of providing ventilation for such items as were used for storing food. When this was undesirable, for instance in the front of an ordinary chest, the 'window' portions were just recessed, leaving the ribs standing up in high releief.

It is sometimes argued that the ecclesiastical appearance of these chests suggests that they were made originally for a church, but this is by no means necessarily the case. That the traceried designs were similar to the work found in churches is true, but it must be remembered the same thing applied to all secular work, because there was no other style than the Gothic. The Gothic style was evolved chiefly from the building of churches, but secular work followed on precisely the same lines.

Renaissance designs   The panel at Fig. 12E is of particular interest in that it shows the beginning of the new spirit the Renaissance brought with it. It is true that there are features about it that are reminiscent of the Gothic, but the main design is something outside what the latter produced. It was probably a case of a man brought up in the Gothic tradition feeling his way rather cautiously in an unfamiliar element. It is somewhat meaningless in the treatment of the upper scrolls terminating in the horizontal band with the leafwork sprouting below, and one has the feeling that here was a man to whom new ideas were suggested but who was uncertain what to make with them.

Romayne panels   Another basic *motif* found in early Renaissance work was the Romayne panel, Fig. 12F, which consisted of a wreath of leafwork encircling the carved representation of a head, usually in profile. Such designs were often found on buildings, for instance, in the Gateway of Hampton Court Palace, and they provided a rich field for the carver's imagination. Sometimes they were purely mythological head pieces, often of Roman origin, the head having the wreath of victory around the brow. On the other hand, these busts were often carved as a portrait of the person for whom the chest was made, and one can imagine the self-sufficiency of the owner as he would point out the likeness to his friends – though to judge from some the result could hardly have been flattering.

We have gone into the details found on these chests at some length because they form the basis upon which ornament of the time was built up. First the Gothic tracery or the linenfold, then the curious intermixture of the Renaissance with the Gothic, and finally the purer Renaissance, if such a term may be applied to a style which was handled in so free a way. Whatever its merits as a design, however, it had this about it, that it was extremely virile and spirited in its execution. A man came across this and that *motif*, and he worked on them with a complacent disregard for their true meaning and gave of his best in dealing with them. The result was production of the Tudor Gothic style.

At this point we may leave the chest for the time being. That made during the last phase of the period, that of Elizabeth, was similar to that in Fig. 7, except that the linenfold device was replaced by Renaissance details, and the framing was usually more or less elaborately carved. We shall pick up the thread again when we come to the next chapter dealing with the Jacobean period.

Settles, chairs, and stools

It has been noted already that the chest was often used as a seat, and at a time when furniture was scarce one can understand that it would

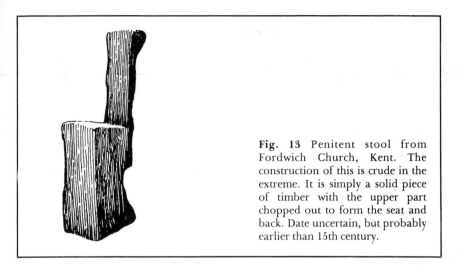

Fig. 13 Penitent stool from Fordwich Church, Kent. The construction of this is crude in the extreme. It is simply a solid piece of timber with the upper part chopped out to form the seat and back. Date uncertain, but probably earlier than 15th century.

conveniently fulfil the purpose. Just what the first chair was like is doubtful. I came across the curious Penitent stool, Fig. 13, in the old church at Fordwich, in Kent, and it may be that a similar structure was used for secular purposes. It is a solid block of oak with a sort of huge notch cut in it to form a seat. The church itself dates from before the Norman Conquest, though the date of the stool itself is uncertain.

The earliest form of seating accommodation was probably evolved from the early planked chest as suggested by the dotted lines in the left hand illustration in Fig. 14. The construction of the two is practically identical, and one can conceive a craftsman of some imagination cutting away the front and back and evolving a long form of the kind in Fig. 15. The only real difference is that in the latter the ends or legs are given a cant to give stability, and are shaped out in Gothic form. Also the long rails are fitted in slots in the legs instead of being nailed to notches at the outside, and the underside is cut away in imitation of the heading of a Gothic arch.

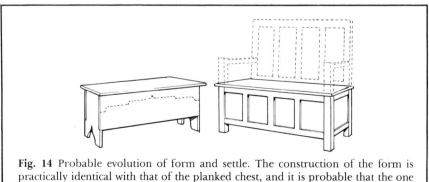

Fig. 14 Probable evolution of form and settle. The construction of the form is practically identical with that of the planked chest, and it is probable that the one was evolved from the other. In the same way the early settle was really only a chest with the posts and back continued upwards.

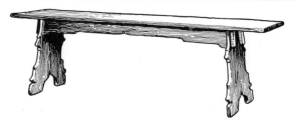

Fig. 15 Long form with Gothic shapings. This was the usual seating accommodation for the majority of people. In a hall there might be one chair, the seat of honour for the principal person (hence the term 'chairman') but forms or stools were good enough for the others. Early 16th century.

Fig. 16 A and **B** simple Tudor Gothic stools. Note that the Gothic shaping of the uprights at **B** is similar to that in the long form in Fig. 15. Early 16th century. **C** Elizabethan box stool. A small box space is formed beneath the seat, the latter acting as a lid. Late 16th century.

The two stools in Fig. 16A and B show clearly this stage of development. That to the left is entirely of the planked chest formation, whilst the other has the refinements already noted in the use of slots to contain the side rails and the shaping of the rails and legs.

Just as the framed-up chest replaced the planked type, so a framed construction came to be used for stools. The method used for the one probably gave the suggestion for the other. Fig. 16C shows a stool of this type, and it is interesting to note that the chest idea is still retained in that a box is formed beneath the seat. The carved flutes partly filled with nullings are a feature that was used considerably in Elizabethan times and in the following century.

Fig. 17 Settle with chest accommodation. A settle of this kind is really just a chest with the back and arms continued up at the top. Mid. 16th century.

Settles Returning to Fig. 14 it will be seen that the development of the settle from the framed-up chest is suggested. It seems a likely theory that this is what happened. The disadvantage of using a chest as a seat must have become obvious, and as men began to make their houses more comfortable and were able to afford more luxury it probably occurred to someone that by suitable adaptation the chest could be made far more comfortable. It meant merely that the back posts would have to be continued up to enable a back framing to be added, and the front posts taken up high enough to provide support for the arms.

The result was the form of settle shown in Fig. 17, which is virtually just a chest with the back and arms above it. The chest portion is retained with the seat acting as a lid. It seems that sometimes the chest was omitted, as shown in Fig. 18, though even here the panelled front is

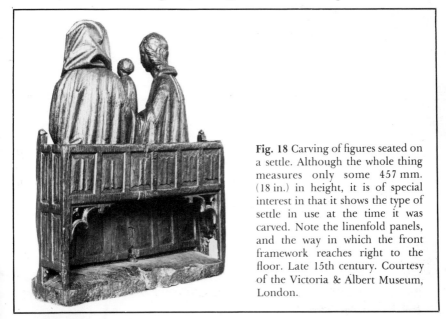

Fig. 18 Carving of figures seated on a settle. Although the whole thing measures only some 457 mm. (18 in.) in height, it is of special interest in that it shows the type of settle in use at the time it was carved. Note the linenfold panels, and the way in which the front framework reaches right to the floor. Late 15th century. Courtesy of the Victoria & Albert Museum, London.

retained. This would be done partly from convention, and partly because it helped to keep away draughts which must have been strongly in evidence in early houses. This illustration is from a small piece of carving cut out of a solid block, and now in South Kensington Museum, and its chief interest from our point of view lies in its showing the form of settle used in the late fifteenth century.

As furniture became more plentiful, and there was no longer the rigid need for economy, the chest portion was eliminated entirely, the under-portion being made up of an open framing of turned legs and stretchers.

Evolution of the chair   The development of the chair was identical with that of the settle. It was really just a short chest or box with back and arms above it. That in Fig. 19 shows the early type. It is not suggested that this was the earliest form of chair (forgetting the Fordwich example, Fig. 13), but that the evolution of the domestic chair came about in this way. There is, of course, the famous coronation chair in Westminster Abbey which dates back to the fourteenth century, and there are several other early Gothic chairs in churches and halls in various parts of the country, but these were made for special purposes and cannot be classed in any way as domestic pieces.

By omitting the lower box portion the chair became less cumbersome and, as we have noted, the need for economy was not of such importance. A particularly fine example dating from the end of the Tudor Gothic period is that in Fig. 20. It now stands in the museum at South Kensington, and there are several features worth examining.

Firstly, the back is given a backward rake, a detail that soon occurred to the carpenters once the idea of a chair had been thought of. At first the back had been continued straight up (see the settle in Fig. 18), but any one who has sat in a straight-backed church pew for any length of time will appreciate how really uncomfortable this can become, and a similar conviction must have come into the minds of the early carpenters – or possibly the people who had the chairs made. Consequently the back was made to slope, but the legs were still kept upright, probably because the old convention derived from the chest structure did not suggest the desirability of giving them a corresponding slope.

It is surely a rather remarkable thing that for the whole of the sixteenth century, and for the better part of the next, chairs were still made with straight, upright back legs. One would imagine that it would occur to a man leaning back in a chair that some means might be invented of preventing the chair from tilting right back. It is true that the Elizabethan chairs were heavy, and this would certainly help to counterbalance the weight, but even so there must have been the tendency for a man to topple over backwards, especially when leaning back after a meal, during which the flagon might have passed freely. In the later years of the seventeenth century the heaviness of the chair was no longer an argument, for the chairs had become incomparably lighter and the height of the back had increased!

Fig. 19 Early form of panelled chair with lower box portion. The general form is similar to that of the settle shown in **Fig. 17,** and the idea was probably prompted by the chest. The back in this case has a slight slope, though in many similar chairs it was quite upright. First half 16th century.

Fig. 20 Panelled back chair decorated with inlay and carving. A big advancement on the previous chair. The lower part is open, and the arms are unpanelled. The back has a definite incline, and, although back legs are upright, they are made extra thick at the bottom to give good stability. About 1600.

Fig. 21. Inlaid and carved oak chair. Note that, although the back slopes, there is no rake to the back legs. Early 17th century.

However, there it was, and in returning to the Elizabethan chair in Fig. 20 we find in it a detail showing that the possibility of an accident had occurred to its maker, in that the lower ends of the back legs are made extra thick at the back to help to prevent the chair from tilting backwards. It was probably the germ of the idea which resulted later in the legs being splayed outwards, though, as we say, it took a long time for it to develop. Fig. 21 is another chair similar in type.

Use of inlay The ornamentation of the back brings to notice a form of decoration not yet mentioned, which came into great popularity during

34

the second half of the sixteenth century, that of inlay. This was carried out entirely in the solid. That is, the background was carved out to receive the shaped inlays. All kinds of native woods were used, apple, pear, holly, cherry, and bog oak, and the design, as in the present example, was usually a conventional treatment of naturalesque *motifs*. Occasionally geometrical designs were used. The solid method should be noted in particular, because later on an entirely different system was evolved.

The shaped arms, terminating in semi-scrolled fronts, are of the kind invariably used in Elizabethan chairs, and it may be noted that chairs without arms are exceptional in the period. It is just another example of how ideas will cling on. Possibly it was felt that the arms gave a certain dignity to the person using the chair, for these were still reserved for the more important people, though they were becoming more plentiful.

Tables

The table is a fairly obvious piece of furniture. It is required for all kinds of purposes in the house, though its chief function is for use when dining. One of the earliest surviving specimens are the huge trestle tables at Penshurst Hall, Kent. They date from the fourteenth century, when it was still the custom for the entire household to dine together in the great hall. One would be placed across the upper end of the hall, usually on a raised dais, and another, or sometimes two, at right angles to it, going lengthwise along the hall. The more important guests used the raised one, and the retainers were accommodated at the others in rotation, the serfs sitting at the lower end.

These trestle tables were generally made with movable tops, so that they could be taken to pieces and stored away when the floor space was required to be cleared. They were extremely massive in build, with tops of 100 mm. (4 in.) or so in thickness, supported by heavy trestles or pedestals. The illustration of the hall at Penshurst Place on page 18 shows these tables.

When, as the years passed, men sought more privacy there arose a demand for smaller tables which could be used in the smaller private room in which the family took their meals. The rise, too, of the merchant class brought about the erection of vast numbers of smaller houses, and so there have survived a fair number of smaller tables dating from the sixteenth century. The term 'smaller' is used comparatively. Actually they usually measure 1·8 m. to 2·7 m. (6 ft. to 9 ft.) or 3 m. (10 ft.) in length.

At the end of the fifteenth century and the beginning of the next the Gothic tradition was still strong, and tables were often still of the trestle kind shown in Fig. 22. It will be noted that the rails are held to the trestles with wedges, so that the whole thing could be stacked away when not required in use. It is interesting to compare the Gothic shaping of the trestles with that of the small stool in Fig. 16B.

Fig. 22 Trestle table with Gothic lines. These tables were made specially so that they could be taken to pieces and stacked away flat. The withdrawal of the wedges enabled the rails to be pulled away clear of the trestle ends. First half 16th century.

Fig. 23 Draw-table of Gothic type. The leaves beneath the main top draw outwards to form an extension. Early 16th century. Photograph by courtesy of the Victoria & Albert Museum, London.

Fig. 24 Draw table of Elizabeth's day. This is the earliest form of extending table, and still the most reliable. The extending leaves rest beneath the main top, and as they are pulled out they are caused to rise by means of tapering bearers beneath. Second half 16th century.

The tendency to use a framed-up construction already mentioned in connection with the chest is seen in the next stage of the table, when an underframing of four or six legs joined by rails (such as in the present-day table) was used. Fig. 23 shows an interesting table dating from the opening years of the sixteenth century. It has square legs with the corners chamfered, and the top rails are shaped on the underside with the Gothic arch formation. The long form also shown has this shaping – in fact it is a companion to the table of which we are speaking. Its most interesting feature, however, is that it is of the 'draw' type; that is, it is provided with extending leaves which, contained beneath the top when not required, can be drawn out, so increasing the size of the top considerably.

Bulbous turnings   The draw table of the Elizabethan period is shown in Fig. 24, and the feature that at once strikes one are the heavy bulbous legs. These represent a fashion in turning that had the most amazing popularity in Elizabethan times and in the first half of the seventeenth century. Turning had been introduced in Britain during the sixteenth century, though it does not appear to have been widely used until about the middle of the century. One imagines that the turners, having acquired the technique, decided to make the most of what they had learnt, for there is nothing really logical about such disproportionate legs. The strength of the leg is governed by its thinnest part, so that the heavy bulbous part is entirely wasted from the constructional point of view.

In the particular table shown in Fig. 24 the legs are plain, direct from the lathe, but in most cases they were elaborately carved with nullings, scrolled acanthus leafwork, and other details, as shown on the turnings in the Court cupboard in Fig. 30. Possibly this is another reason why they appealed to the Elizabethans; they offered such scope for decorative detail.

37

Fig. 25 Staircase at the Charterhouse, London. This shows the fine, massive sort of staircases erected in mansions during Elizabeth's reign. Its interest from the point of view of furniture is that it exemplifies the love of decoration that the craftsmen had at the time. The quality of the work, though somewhat crude judged by later standards, is extraordinarily virile and thorough. This staircase was completely destroyed by fire during the bombing of London in the Second World War. Second half 16th century.

Fig. 26 Tudor Gothic fireplace. Early 16th century. The arched stone opening is Gothic, but early Renaissance detail appears in the panelled woodwork.

In most cases the stretcher rails ran round the four sides of the table in the same way as the rails at the top, but occasionally the H arrangement in Fig. 24 is found. In other types two legs only were used, these being built into the centre of the end rails and fitted with cross pieces at the bottom. They were a revival of the pedestal leg used in Gothic times, as exemplified by the Penshurst table on page 18, except that the bottom was joined by a stretcher and the top had a framing to contain the mechanism of the extension.

Cupboards and side tables

It is a rather curious reflection that so many years should have passed without men having devised any means of locking things away privately except in a chest. It tells its own story, that they should have preferred to use something which could be used conveniently for travelling. Once they came to establish their homes on a more convenient basis, however, the necessity for cabinets to hold valuable or private papers, and cupboards to store various other items became felt. Thus wall furniture became increasingly common.

Fig. 27 Side table with Gothic details. A piece such as this would probably have stood in the dining hall of a manor house. It is virtually a chest with the corner posts made extra long to form legs. The Gothic tracery designs carved in the panels are pierced right through. Early 16th century. By courtesy of the Victoria & Albert Museum.

The early form of side table is given in Fig. 27, a piece dating from about 1500 or soon after. It is virtually a chest, with the corner posts continued dowwards to raise it well up from the floor. This was probably its origin. Not that a man, having a chest, would decide that by lengthening the posts he could evolve a sideboard, but that the method of construction was automatically adopted once the idea of a sideboard was thought about. There was probably a subconscious connection between the two ideas, so that it is likely that there was a direct evolution from one to the other. The side table exemplifies the use of the pierced panel, and another point that will appeal to practical readers is the use of the 'mason's mitre' in the moulding surrounding the panel. The use of this is explained more fully in Fig. 37.

Another kind of furniture of the early Tudor Gothic period was the cupboard pure and simple as shown in Fig. 28. It is of the simplest possible construction, consisting of so many boards pegged together and held by the angle plates and strap hinges. Often such cupboards had panels pierced with Gothic tracery designs such as those given at Fig. 12A and B. In fact A is taken from an old cupboard of the kind. Their purpose was probably to hold food, as the pierced panels gave ventilation.

Of a similar type, but of infinitely better construction, is the cupboard shown in Fig. 29. In place of the planks is a framing of four posts, joined by rails with grooves around their edges to hold panels. Here the last-named are pierced and carved in the form of Gothic windows.

The Court cupboard   The development in Elizabethan times is shown in the Court cupboard in Fig. 30. This is worthy of a few moments' attention because it contains many typical features of the period. It was a

Fig. 28 Tudor Gothic planked hutch. This early form of cupboard was made by single planks nailed or pegged together. Early 16th century.

Fig. 29 Framed-up Tudor Gothic hutch. Made by a much improved method to that used for Fig. 28. Here the framework has panels fitting in grooves. First half 16th century.

cupboard which became extremely popular, probably because it gave good accommodation and there was excellent scope for decorative treatment. Note first the lower doors with their three-panel arrangement. Apart from strength, this had the advantage of keeping the panel width down, and so saving the necessity of jointing up. The framing is channel-moulded; that is a shallow groove moulded at the sides is worked along the centre of each member.

Incidentally, whilst on the subject of mouldings, it should be noted that in every case they are worked in the solid, the substance of the framing being moulded. It is mentioned here in particular because it will be seen in the next chapter that the tendency in the following century was to use applied mouldings instead.

Fig. 30 Elizabethan court cupboard. This exemplifies well the love of Elizabethan craftsmen for ornament of every kind. The upper recessed portion is inlaid with various woods such as apple, holly, cherry, bog oak, and stained woods. The carving is typical of the time, being virile, deep and bold if somewhat barbaric in execution. Note the use of the full bulbous turnings richly carved with acanthus leafwork and other conventional details. Late 16th century.

Fig. 31 Buffet with bulbous turnings. This was the Elizabethan form of sideboard. The modern dinner wagon is of similar formation. Often a drawer was fitted beneath the top, the rail acting as the drawer front. Late 16th century.

Attention has already been drawn to the bulbous turnings and their elaborate carving, Fig. 30, and we may now turn to the upper cupboard portion with its sloping sides. It was probably the desire to make space for the bulbous turnings that prompted the cutting away of the cupboard, and at the same time to provide a useful standing space at each side. It will be found that when, later, turning began to decline, the upper cupboard became rectangular in shape, being just set back a few inches from the line of the lower cupboard. Eventually the turnings disappeared almost entirely, being replaced by single drop turnings – but this will be discussed further in chapter 3. It is mentioned here because it helps to explain the reason for the shape of the upper cupboard. The carving in the frieze is a typical Elizabethan detail which continued into the seventeenth century.

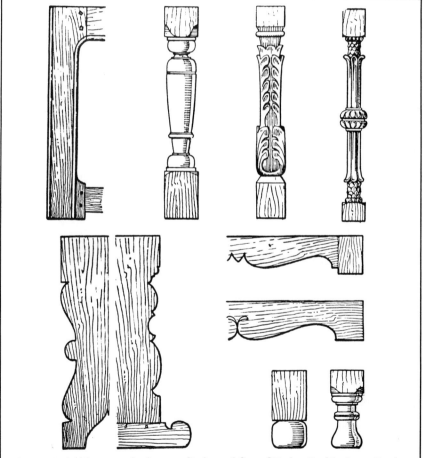

Fig. 32 Typical legs, trestle shapes, plinths and feet of Tudor Gothic times. To the above might be added the full bulbous turning, usually carved, which became so popular in Elizabethan days. Typical examples of this are given in **Fig. 24, 30** and **31**. 16th century.

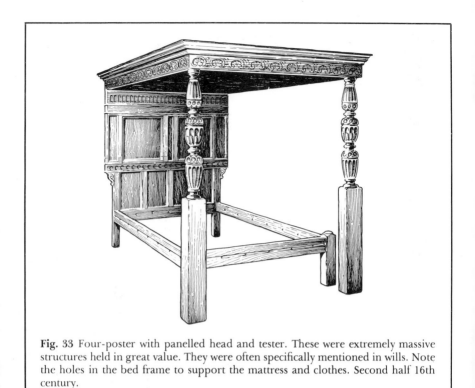

Fig. 33 Four-poster with panelled head and tester. These were extremely massive structures held in great value. They were often specifically mentioned in wills. Note the holes in the bed frame to support the mattress and clothes. Second half 16th century.

Bedsteads

Sleeping arrangements in the early years were of the simplest and most primitive form for everyone except the chief persons in the household. The fifteenth century saw considerable improvements in this respect, though it was not until the next century that beds became at all common. There were two kinds, the panelled head and foot which was very like the modern form of wood bed, and the four-poster. The last-named developed into a really amazing structure in the time of Elizabeth. That the rooms were abominably draughty is the probable reason for its popularity. The tester or panelling above the bed was hung all round with curtains, so that the sleeper was literally lying in a little room built within the main bedroom. It must have been close and unhealthy, but presumably people preferred that to draughts.

That great importance was attached to these bedsteads is shown by the frequent reference made to them in old wills, and in view of the amount of work put into them they must have been costly things to produce. That in Fig. 33 contains features found in most old beds. Note that the bed frame itself is separate at the foot from the front posts. This was usual in Elizabethan beds, though towards the end of the century the tendency was to join them up.

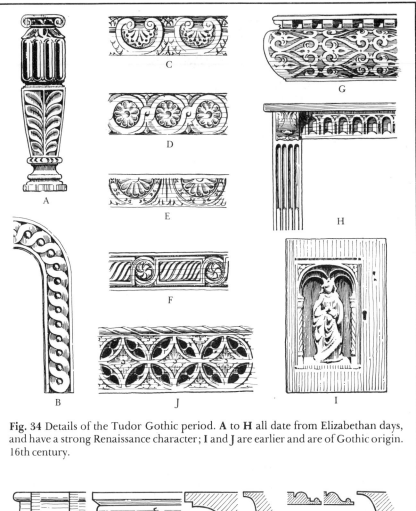

Fig. 34 Details of the Tudor Gothic period. **A** to **H** all date from Elizabethan days, and have a strong Renaissance character; **I** and **J** are earlier and are of Gothic origin. 16th century.

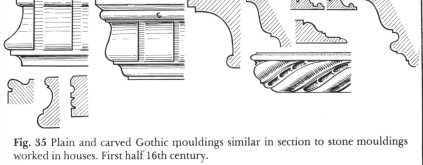

Fig. 35 Plain and carved Gothic mouldings similar in section to stone mouldings worked in houses. First half 16th century.

Fig. 34, 35, and 36 will prove of particular interest to practical cabinet makers and draughtsmen, though they are well worthy of the attention of all students because the sections of mouldings and carved details are extremely important factors when dating a period piece.

45

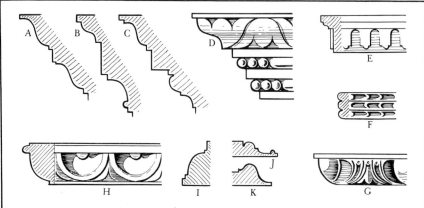

Fig. 36 Examples of Elizabethan mouldings; mostly crude copies of classical section. Second half 16th century.

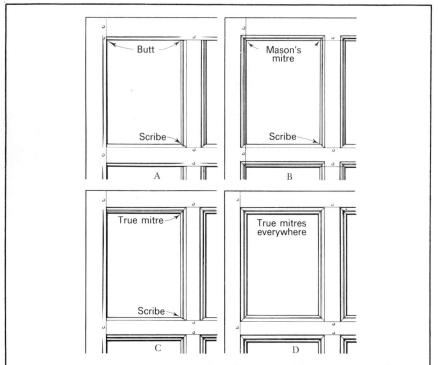

Fig. 37 How the true mitre was evolved. At first the mouldings were merely butted (cut off square) at the ends of rails as at **A**, the beads on the uprights being run out opposite the joints. Later the mitre used in stone work was copied, in which the mitre was carved in the solid in one of the pieces as at **B**. Later came the true mitre, as at **C** and **D**. Note, however, that at **A, B,** and **C** the top edge of the rail is chamfered, another copy of stone work in which it was formed to allow water to drain away easily. The moulding of the uprights was merely scribed, that is, cut at a corresponding angle to fit over it.

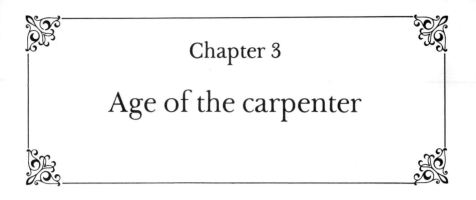

Chapter 3

Age of the carpenter

Jacobean period

This chapter carries us from the beginning of the house of Stuart in 1603 until the end of the Commonwealth in 1660. So far as domestic furniture was concerned, except for certain smaller details and a few innovations, it differed little from that of Elizabeth's reign. The same wood (oak) was used, the Renaissance was still the source from which ideas were taken, and the quality of the work was similar. It is dealt with in a separate chapter, however, because it was the last phase in a certain definite technique. Vast changes were at hand, the greatest that have ever overtaken furniture throughout its history, and it is therefore natural that one should pause and give special emphasis to a style which had run its course and was to become as dead as the proverbial doornail.

However, these changes are dealt with particularly in chapter 4, and our present purpose is to see what sort of furniture men were making when James the Sixth of Scotland became the First of England, and during the troublous years that followed, culminating in the declaration of the Commonwealth. It may be objected that Charles II was also a Stuart Monarch, and that his period should be included in this chapter. The changes just mentioned, however, began during his reign, so that although all Charles II furniture is, strictly speaking, Jacobean, much of it is usually referred to as 'Early Walnut,' because of the marked differences in style. The terminology is one of style rather than one of period.

The accession of James did not make a great deal of difference in the lives of the majority of the populace. The stirring spirit of the Renaissance was still a great influence, if in rather diminished form, and people's endeavour to make their homes more comfortable continued. The journeys of discovery and conquest during Elizabeth's reign had opened up a new source of wealth, trading had increased tremendously (itself a source of wealth and, equally important, to a new class), and these coinciding with the coming of the Renaissance gave encouragement to the domestic arts.

Fig. 1 Oak staircase in Hatfield House, early 17th century. Compare with Fig. 25, page 38.

The outbreak of war in Charles I reign must have acted as a strong brake on the progress of things, yet it was not so marked as one might have imagined. The probable explanation is that it was largely local in its effect. A campaign in the north might turn men's thoughts locally from making, or having made, things for their houses, but in even an adjoining county people might know little of what was happening owing to lack of easy transit. Then, again, during the winter months little was possible in the way of military activities, so that altogether there was more time for craftsmanship than might at first be imagined.

Cromwell's short Protectorship of eleven years or so helped to restore the trade which had been largely lost. His naval victories opened the seas again to our ships, and this is always one of the finest tonics the domestic arts can have.

Jacobean chairs

The late sixteenth or early seventeenth century chair, as exemplified on page 33, was remarkable more for its massiveness and strength than for its comfort, and its direct successor in Jacobean times was little different. It had a similar formation, with panelled back sloping at an angle, semi-scrolled arms, and turned legs. The back was usually carved with various conventional designs of leaf and flower work, arcadings, or a geometrical pattern; Fig. 2 is a typical example. Note that the scrolled cresting still lies above the uprights and that the ear pieces are retained. Chairs of this kind continued to be made throughout the Jacobean period and in country districts until the close of the seventeenth century.

There were, however, changes at hand. It is obvious that for a chair of the type in Fig. 2 to have any comfort at all it would have to be provided

Fig. 2 Panelled-back chair and framed stool. The construction of the chair is practically identical with that shown in **Fig. 20**, page 33, and the general treatment is similar. Note the scrolled cresting and ear pieces. The stool has the baluster-shaped legs popular throughout Jacobean times. First half 17th century.

with a cushion—certainly one for the seat and if possible one for the back. One can imagine a man seated by the fireside closely considering the point, and calling in his carpenter to devise some means of padding the chair. Or possibly a man who had travelled abroad had seen the comfort which foreign countries had attained (they were always before us in this sort of thing), felt something of disgust at the comparatively barbaric state of things which still maintained here, and so set his craftsmen to work out a new idea.

Beginning of upholstery   However this may be, it was during the reign of James I that the first upholstered chair made its appearance. Possibly the reader may be surprised that the idea had not occurred to men earlier. Upholstery on a chair seems such an obvious thing. It must be remembered that people's outlook on life differs at various periods. What may seem right to one generation may appear to be merely foolish to another. In early days the chair was a seat of honour; there would probably be only one in even a large hall, and a man using it would not look specially to find it comfortable. In fact, anything in the way of comfort was regarded with a certain feeling of contempt and was felt to be effeminate. Shakespeare, in his *Richard III*, makes Buckingham say, 'This prince is not an Edward! He is not lolling on a lewd day-bed.' This day-bed was the counterpart of the modern settee. Presumably, when people were really ill, they stayed in bed. If they got up at all they were expected to go about the ordinary business of the day.

There was something effeminate in the character and habits of James I, and this rapidly showed itself in the Royal court: its manners, dress, conditions, and so on. As a consequence there was a general tendency for men to have a less Spartan-like outlook, and an immediate consequence so far as furniture was concerned was the introduction of the upholstered chair.

One of the finest collections of chairs of this type, dating from the early seventeenth century, is that at Knole House, near Sevenoaks. Many rooms in this old mansion were refurnished in preparation for a visit by James I, and vast numbers of chairs were made for the purpose. They form an interesting example of how men, once they like an idea, will fly to extremes, for practically every portion of the woodwork is covered with material, even the legs, which obviously would not in any way add to the comfort of the chair.

A popular innovation or rather revival, for the type had been in use earlier, was the X chair, an example of which is given in Fig. 4. The reason for the name is obvious from the general formation. Note how every part of the framing is covered with material. It is, in fact, very like the collection of chairs at Knole. The provision of the footstool is typical.

It will be realized that upholstered chairs of this kind might be well enough in a great mansion or palace, but would not stand up to the everyday use of busy households in a humbler state of life. These needed something sturdier, and Fig. 3 is an example of the sort of upholstered

Fig. 3

Fig. 4

Fig. 3 Armchair covered with Turkey work. In this we see the early beginning of the upholstered chair, though in itself it can hardly claim to be upholstered. It is little more than a covering stretched over the framework. First half 17th century.

Fig. 4 Example of the X pattern chair. This is a type of chair that became popular during James I reign. At Knole Park, Kent, large numbers of these chairs, made specially in honour of a visit paid by James I, still exist. Early 17th century.

chair that would have been found in the average well-to-do house. Not that all the chairs were of this kind; there might not be more than one or two in a whole house, the majority being of the plain wood type, but such upholstered chairs that did exist were mostly of this kind.

Fig. 6 Farthingale chair of James I time. This illustration is intended to show the way in which costume affected the design of the chair. The huge farthingale dress made impossible the use of the armchair of the type shown in **Fig. 2**. Early 17th century.

Farthingale chairs   We have at this period an interesting example of how costume came to influence the design of furniture. The fashion of the time dictated that ladies should wear the huge farthingale dress, and one can imagine how awkward it must have been for a lady to sit down in an armchair of the kind in, say, Fig. 2. So the farthingale chair came into being, of which an example is given in Fig. 6. The absence of arms allows the dress to spread out at each side without hindrance. The X chair in Fig. 4 would serve the purpose equally well, since there is a deep, loose cushion above the upholstered seat and the arms are low.

Two chairs probably made during the Cromwellian period are shown in Fig. 5. They are of a sound, thoroughly reliable form that would stand up to the hardest wear. That to the left has a covering of leather so thin that it can scarcely be called upholstery, held on with large roundhead nails, and the front legs have the bobbin turning very popular at the time. The other has a wooden seat, and a point worthy of note is the open back with slats. This marks one more step in the progress of the chair from its heavy, massive formation to the light proportions it was eventually to assume. Note that in both chairs the back legs are still upright and that the stretcher rails are retained, although in that to the right the front one is raised from its former lower position level with the side rails.

The settle   Whilst on the subject of chairs, it may be noted that the settle was still made in country districts. The farmhouse in particular usually

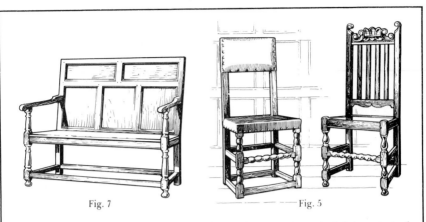

Fig. 7

Fig. 5

Fig. 5 Cromwellian and Yorkshire type chairs. The example to the left is typical of the plainer sort of chair made during the Commonwealth. It has a stout leather covering stretched over the framework. The other chair is characteristic of the kind made in Yorkshire or Derbyshire. Mid 17th century.

Fig. 7 The settle in Jacobean times. The settle in **Fig. 17**, page 31, should be compared with this. Note how the lower portion is completely open and has turned legs. First half 17th century.

Fig. 8 Combined table, settle, and chest. The rarity of domestic furniture is shown by this piece which served three distinct purposes. These are popularly known as 'monks' benches', though there is not the slightest connection between them and monks. Mid 17th century.

had its settle, Fig. 7, the sturdy construction and plain form making it more suitable for the rougher conditions inevitable in the country. Another similar piece was that which for some unknown reason has been given the curious title of 'monk's bench,' though what its possible connection with monks can be is difficult to understand! We refer of course to the settle with the movable back, which was made to tilt and slide forward, so forming a table. The example in Fig. 8 shows this

Fig. 9 Dining-table with baluster turned legs and carved rails. The general tendency in the 17th century was to replace the heavy, bulbous turnings of Elizabeth's reign with a lighter kind. The carving in the legs was also invariably omitted. In this example the top rails are decorated with lunette carving, and the angles are filled in with carved spandrels. Mid 17th century.

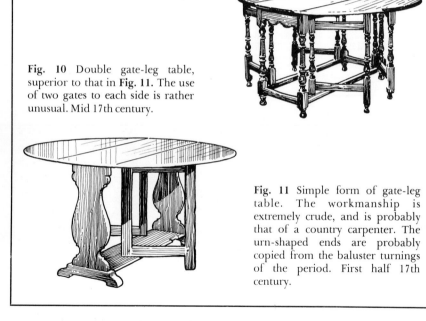

Fig. 10 Double gate-leg table, superior to that in Fig. 11. The use of two gates to each side is rather unusual. Mid 17th century.

Fig. 11 Simple form of gate-leg table. The workmanship is extremely crude, and is probably that of a country carpenter. The urn-shaped ends are probably copied from the baluster turnings of the period. First half 17th century.

feature, and it will also be seen that the lower portion is in the form of a chest, the lid of which forms the seat. Lunette carving, such as that on the rails, was a favourite form of decoration.

Tables of the seventeenth century (first half)

The Elizabethan table, either of the draw or fixed top type, continued with little variety in form during the reigns of the early Stuarts and Cromwellian times. The legs were of the heavy bulbous turned kind,

Fig. 12 Interior showing large dining-table. Compare with **Fig. 9.**

generally carved, though the tendency as the seventeenth century progressed was to thin down the turning and omit the carving. In the full bulbous early Jacobean leg extra pieces were glued on at all four sides to provide wood for the required thickness. This can be seen clearly in the table in Fig. 24, page 37, in which the squares at top and bottom of the legs show the original thickness of the wood. Later Jacobean legs were usually no thicker than could be turned from the squares of wood with no extra applied pieces. Fig. 9 shows a table dating from about the middle of the seventeenth century with turned baluster legs of this kind. Another table similar in type is shown in Fig. 12.

Up to this time the chief, and practically only use of a table was that of dining, and now that people were settling into a more comfortable way of living the usefulness of a smaller form of table must have become felt. For instance, in the smaller private rooms a huge draw table was unnecessary, yet some form of table was essential. Again, in the smaller houses there would not be room for the large dining table. The result was the gateleg table, with its circular, oval, or rectangular top divided into three pieces, the centre one of which was fixed to the main framework, the others being hinged to it.

That in Fig. 10 is an example of the better kind, the legs being turned and the whole thing framed together with mortise and tenon joints. A cruder example is that in Fig. 11, in which the uprights are merely solid pieces with a rather crude shaping cut at the sides.

Fig. 13 Carved oak open-tiered buffet. This is the early form of sideboard used to hold dishes and the like in the dining room. First half 17th century. Photograph by courtesy of the Victoria & Albert Museum.

Fig. 14 Court cupboard in Jacobean times. An interesting comparison can be made with the cupboard Fig. 30, page 42. Note the substitution of thinner and plain turnings in the upper storey. Mid 17th century.

Fig. 15 Farmhouse dresser with plate rack. Although made in oak there are features which suggest the walnut period, specially in the shaped headings to the upper cupboards. The turned legs, however, are purely Jacobean. Second half 17th century.

Various cabinets

There were two kinds of cabinets chiefly in use in Jacobean dining-rooms, the Court cupboard and the buffet, with its three tiers open at all sides, Fig. 13. Both of these came into use in Elizabethan times, and we now come to the form they took in the seventeenth century. It is instructive to turn to the Elizabethan example of a Court cupboard on page 42 and compare it with its Jacobean counterpart in Fig. 14. In the former the upper stage is canted at the sides, and the turnings are of the full bulbous kind, richly carved all over. In the later example the upper stage is rectangular and is recessed only slightly, and the turnings are considerably smaller and are plain. In this they follow the tendency already noted in regard to the legs of tables. As the century progressed the turnings became mere pendants beneath the frieze without reaching down to the lower part of the cabinet. This was the final stage of the Court cupboard. It died a natural death during the second half of the century, for it was essentially a piece for the well-to-do and when walnut came into popularity it just disappeared.

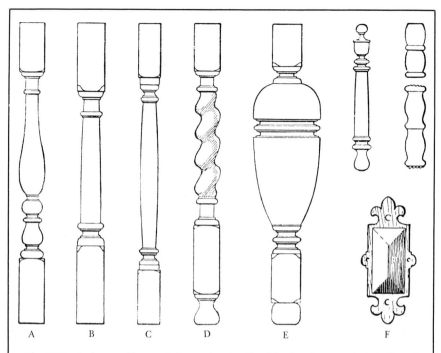

A   B   C   D   E   F

Fig. 16 Typical turned legs and decorative details of the Jacobean period. **A, B,** and **C** are plain turnings of the kind usually fitted to gate-leg tables. **A** is the urn shape from which the flat shaping in the table in **Fig. 11** was probably taken; **D** is a twist turning; **E** the full bulbous shape which is a survival of Elizabethan times; **F** some half-turnings and a raised pattern with fretted background which show the tendency to use applied decoration.

It was in a different class from the dresser, which belonged more to the farmhouse, and which continued to be made even throughout the eighteenth century. Such a dresser is given in Fig. 15. It may be noted in passing that this was evolved directly from the side table of the kind shown on page 40. There was no upper staging of shelves, the latter being added later when plates and dishes became more plentiful.

A smaller item that may be mentioned here is the Bible box, see Fig. 18. Every family of any note had its Bible in those days, and it was a most treasured possession. A place in which it could be kept safely was desirable, hence the various small boxes which have survived. Some of them were provided with a stand and a sloping lid upon which the Bible could rest at a convenient angle when being read. In the finer specimens the fronts were carved with the usual conventional floral work as in the examples given.

Occasionally one finds the interior of these boxes fitted up, probably for the purpose of holding deeds and other valuable papers. It is possible that some were intended specifically for the purpose of writing, but against this there is the fact that few people could write in the seventeenth

Fig. 17 Staircase at Knole Park, Sevenoaks. Although still of massive formation, this staircase is somewhat lighter than the Elizabethan example in **Fig.** 25, page 38. Note that the balusters are turned and free from carving, a general tendency in Jacobean times. Their shape 'can be compared with the Jacobean table shown on page 54. Early 17th century.

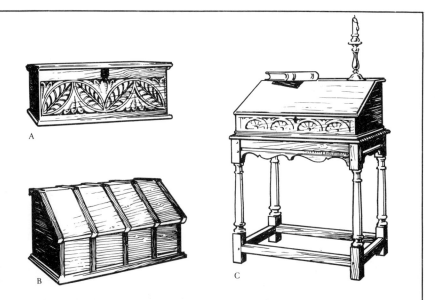

Fig. 18 Small Bible boxes and desks. The object of the sloping lid was probably to provide a convenient rest for the Bible when being read, though it is possible that some were intended for writing. 17th century.

Fig. 19 Jacobean panels with applied mouldings.

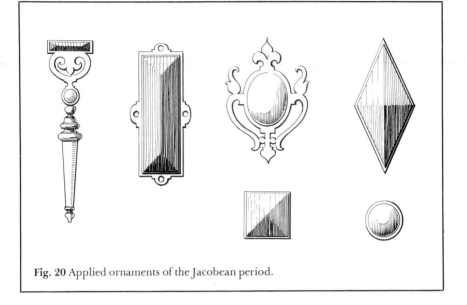

Fig. 20 Applied ornaments of the Jacobean period.

century, and it would have been most uncomfortable to write at, being far too high. Reading was the more probable purpose of the sloping top, any writing that was done being incidental.

The chest

Although many new forms of furniture had been evolved from the chest, the latter was extraordinarily persistent in retaining its popularity more or less in its original form. It continued to be made in large numbers throughout the seventeenth century, and in provincial districts remained as a sort of standard household possession long after oak furniture had gone out of fashion in the towns. The probable explanation was that, for its size, it had maximum accommodation and was as simple a piece of work that a carpenter could undertake. It was not, in fact, until the chest of drawers, with its greater convenience, was invented that it began to decline in popularity.

Fig. 21 is a typical chest of the early years of the seventeenth century. It is well enough made in its way, though the detail is extremely crude when closely examined. It was probably the work of a country carpenter who could make a reasonable job of cutting, say, a mortise and tenon joint, but was rather out of his depth when it came to any carving.

One has to bear things like this in mind when arriving at an opinion on a piece of old furniture. Age may have given it a fine colour and centuries of polishing produced an inimitable surface, but, this apart, the mere fact that it was made in the seventeenth century does not make it beautiful. There were poor workmen then as now.

Fig. 21 Jacobean chest with carved panels. The development from the chest of the previous century can be seen by comparing this with **Fig. 5** and **Fig. 7**, page 23. In this particular example the whole workmanship is particularly crude. First half 17th century.

Chests with drawers   Returning to the chest, we now come to the last phase and its final disappearance – or rather conversion. We have seen how certain pieces such as the side table were evolved from it without affecting the chest itself, this still continuing in its old form, probably with varying detail, but virtually the same. Now, however, it was to lose its identity as a chest, although its use remained unaltered. It came about through the invention of the drawer. The latter was becoming increasingly popular in the seventeenth century, and it probably occurred to someone that the inconvenience of having to turn out the entire contents of a chest in order to reach something at the bottom could be avoided to a large extent if the drawer system were applied to it.

Fig. 22 A Chest with lower drawers. **B** chest of drawers with mitred mouldings. The inconvenience of having to turn out a chest to reach things at the bottom probably prompted the idea of adding drawers as at **A** . They quickly became popular with the result that the entire chest was given over to drawers. 17th century.

These things usually have their beginning in a small way, and the thin end of the wedge can be seen in the left hand chest in Fig. 22, which is virtually just an ordinary chest with two drawers fitted at the bottom. Its advantages must have become immediately apparent, for very shortly the whole of the space was given over to drawers as in the right hand chest in Fig. 22. Once this had happened, the old form of chest which had survived for centuries with practically no change of form became extinct, and it has never again been revived.

Whilst we still have the chest in Fig. 22 in mind, it is worth while noting the method of decoration employed on the drawer fronts. It consists of *applied* mouldings mitred round to form various patterns. It is the fact that they are applied that is specially to be noted, because we saw in the Elizabethan period that they were invariably worked in the solid. This method of applying ornament is typical of the later Jacobean period, and it extends to such details as half-turnings, diamonds, studs, and so on. A group of Jacobean panels with applied mouldings is given in Fig. 19.

The Jacobean bedroom

There were three kinds of bedsteads made in Jacobean times: the four-poster, the panelled head and foot type, and that covered over with fabric and heavily draped. The last-named was an innovation of the early years of the seventeenth century, but it hardly comes under the heading of domestic furniture, because it was the type of thing that would not be made for anyone except a person of the highest quality. There is an example in the famous King's bedroom at Knole. It was made specially for James I during a visit he paid to the mansion, and it is entirely on the lines of the upholstered chairs mentioned earlier in this chapter. Every portion of the woodwork is covered with rich material, and above the tester are four great plumes, one at each corner.

Such a bedstead was well enough in a palace, but was obviously not suitable for use in humbler houses. It is worth noting at this stage, however, because the type became popular again towards the end of the century. The nobleman or rich merchant would use the four-poster bedstead, an Elizabethan example of which was given on page 44. This continued with few alterations except in detail for the greater part of the seventeenth century.

Well-to-do farmers and those of similar standing used the simpler panelled head and foot bedstead. This was practically identical with the modern wood bedstead, except of course that the side rails were of wood and that the mattress was supported by ropes which were threaded through holes bored through the rails. Rather more elaborate specimens had both head and foot made extra high, so to support a simpler tester, as that in Fig. 23. This is virtually three pieces of panelling, with side rails added to support the mattress.

For the other furnishings of the bedroom there was the chest, which

Fig. 23 Simple canopied bedstead with panelled ends of the type used in smaller manor houses or farm houses. Note the holes in the rails and head and foot to take the roping which supported the mattress. Mid 17th century.

Fig. 24 Panelled wardrobe with channelled framing. A typical arrangement of the panelling is shown in the doors. It is similar to that in the court cupboards **Fig. 30**, page 42 and **Fig. 14**, page 56. Note the use of the long horizontal panel in all three examples. 17th century.

later in the period was fitted with one or more drawers, and eventually the complete chest of drawers. In addition, various forms of cupboards or presses made their appearance for the more convenient storing of clothes and linen. Fig. 24 shows an early piece, and was the origin to which the modern wardrobe can be traced.

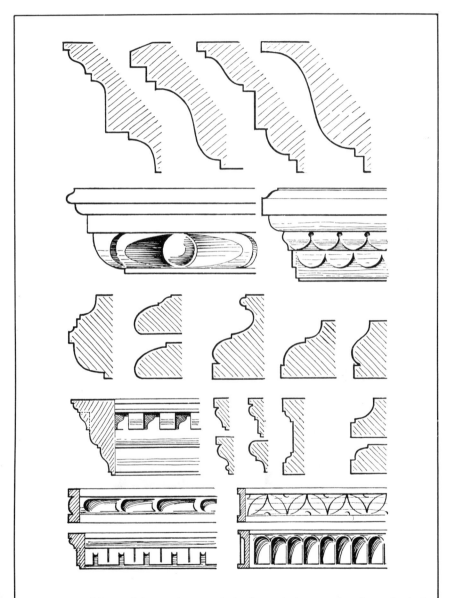

Fig. 25 Mouldings of the Jacobean period. The majority are taken from classical sources though the actual treatment is very free.

Jacobean ornament

This does not differ a great deal from that of the Elizabethan period. It is in the main a rather free rendering of the Renaissance. Certain new features made their appearance – the lozenge panel for instance, which was of diamond shape and was usually ornamented with simple gouge cuts. (See the top panels of the bedstead in Fig. 23.) Such carved details as the guilloche, lunette, and arcaded panels (see page 45) remained popular through Jacobean times.

Later pieces of the period, however, tended to become more artificial, in that decoration was applied rather than worked in the solid. Take, for

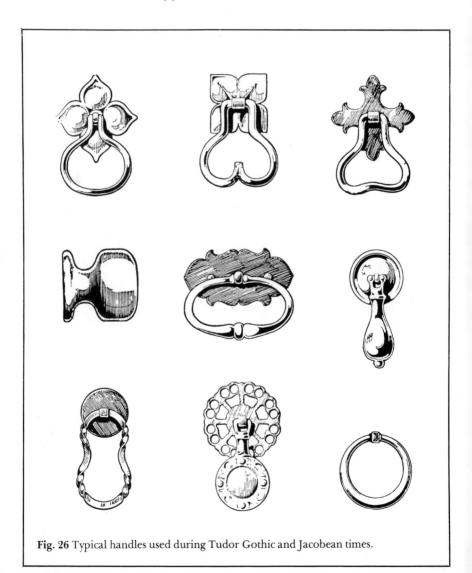

Fig. 26 Typical handles used during Tudor Gothic and Jacobean times.

instance, the group of panels in Fig. 19. In every case the mouldings are applied, and, although there undoubtedly is a certain decorative value in the arrangement, they tend to become somewhat meaningless since they bear no relationship to the construction. In Elizabethan work mouldings were worked at the edges of rails or were channelled along the centre, and have a definite purpose in taking off the harshness of a square edge or enriching a plain surface. In the Jacobean work they often appear to be laid on in any convenient way that suggested itself to the imagination of the craftsman.

The same thing applies to the other decorative details which were invariably applied. A typical group is given in Fig. 20.

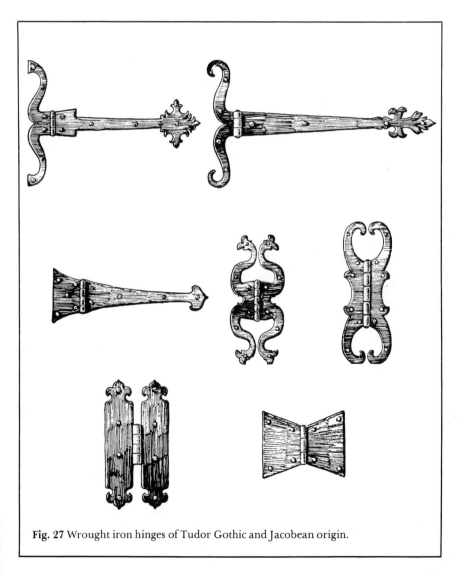

Fig. 27 Wrought iron hinges of Tudor Gothic and Jacobean origin.

Fig. 28 Early Jacobean period fireplace. The Renaissance detail of the woodwork is clearly seen, but the Gothic arched heading of the opening is retained. Late 16th or early 17th century.

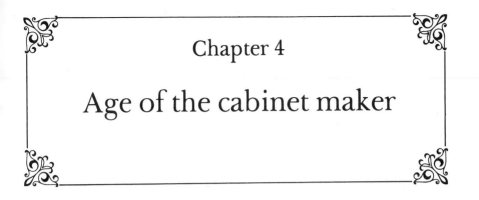

Chapter 4

Age of the cabinet maker

Transitional period

We have already referred to the period beginning with the Restoration in 1660 as being very remarkable so far as furniture was concerned. It certainly was. It was not merely that new ideas of form and decoration were evolved, but that a far more advanced technique of craftsmanship was built up, one which belonged essentially to furniture as distinct from joinery and carpentry. In other words, it was the period when the cabinet maker came into being, the man who specialized in furniture making.

The coincidence of many things brought about the change. The austere habits of people during the Commonwealth underwent something like a revolution when Charles II ascended the throne. It was the swing of the pendulum from simplicity to extravagance. Charles had lived for many years on the Continent, where conditions, so far as the wealthy classes were concerned, were far more luxurious than here, and it was natural that foreign ideas should spread to this country when he came back as monarch. This influence, coming at the same time as the strong reaction already mentioned, set the stage for a new standard of things.

Then again, in a closely following reign another powerful foreign influence made itself felt. William III was a Dutchman who loved the surroundings to which he had been accustomed. Thus in a space of some thirty years two events occurred which laid their mark on the crafts of England.

Thirdly, there was the introduction of walnut as a furniture wood, a material of far finer grain and of a milder nature than oak. It lent itself far more readily to finer workmanship, yet was quite as reliable though it had not the same durable nature. To make a rough analogy, it was like a mason who had known no other medium than a coarse sandstone, being given a piece of fine marble to carve. All sorts of possibilities were opened.

Finally, and possibly most important, there was the introduction of the craft of veneering. As the reader probably knows, this consists of laying a

Fig. 1 Staircase at Longor Hall, Shropshire. There is a marked difference in character between this staircase and that in **Fig. 17**, page 39. The whole thing is lighter and the workmanship is far more refined. About 1670.

thin sheet of wood, usually finely marked, upon a groundwork of a less interesting but thoroughly reliable wood. It was something entirely new and presented all sorts of problems of which there was no previous experience. Whilst, on the one hand, it enabled all sorts of decorative effects to be obtained which could not be carried out in the solid, it necessitated methods of construction, the reliability or otherwise of which could only be proved by time. The craftsmen learnt much from foreign workmen who were already familiar with veneer, but they had a good deal to find out for themselves, and they undoubtedly did make many mistakes, as the large cracked or twisted panels of some of the work of the period show.

Taken all round, then, there were plenty of circumstances to encourage a new departure in style, and it is a thing that is obvious to anyone who makes a comparison between a cabinet made in the traditional oak style and one of walnut of the same period. Be it remembered that many craftsmen continued to work in oak, especially in country districts, right till the end of the seventeenth century and even later.

New methods of construction

As an example, take Fig. 2 and 3, which show two cabinets made within forty years of each other, but of which one is in oak and the other in veneered walnut. The oak piece was made in precisely the same way that all woodwork had been made for the past century or two. The maker recognized the inevitability of shrinkage and accordingly framed-up the parts, working grooves at the edges in which the panels were free to shrink. This is shown in both the doors and the sides, where the panels stand in from the level of the framework in line with the grooves.

The joints of the frames are pegged to hold them together (joints were invariably put together dry, without glue) and, to relieve the plainness, a channelling is worked along practically every rail and stile. The finish of the wood is uneven, many of the panels showing plane marks and the edges being anything but straight.

Now turn to the walnut cabinet and note how impossible it would be to apply these methods of construction. In the first place the doors are flat over their entire surface, what panelled appearance there is being effected by the application of a cross-banding of veneer. The same thing applies to the sides which are flat. It is obvious that a panel fitting loosely in the grooves of a framework could not possibly be used.

Furthermore, a pegged joint put together dry would not be practical because the slightest movement would cause the veneer to split. Then in regard to the channelling, if this were worked it would necessarily cut right through the veneer and expose the groundwork beneath. As for the finish, it can be taken as essential that the groundwork must be prepared perfectly. The slightest blemish in it shows through to the surface of the veneer and, even though the latter may be laid to look tolerably well at the time, it will eventually part company with the groundwork and cause all sorts of complications after a year or so. In any case, walnut was given a far more highly polished surface than oak, so that the effect of an uneven surface would be like that of a badly distorted mirror.

It is not possible in one short chapter to give *all* the reasons why a new technique in furniture construction became necessary, but these few points are sufficient to show the fundamental causes of the change. As we say, these early cabinet makers did make mistakes, the lesson of which their followers of the eighteenth century were to profit by, but when one considers the vastness of the change and the short time in which it was carried out, it was on the whole remarkably successful.

Changes in design   Turning to the walnut cabinet in Fig. 3 again, and comparing it with, say, the Court cupboard in Fig. 14, page 56, one is struck by the vastly different method by which the decorative appearance is obtained. The oak cupboard is carved and moulded everywhere. The wood is just a medium for the carving and there are no large unbroken surfaces. The doors, for instance, are subdivided into small panels – in fact, the whole effect is obtained by the constant change in the level of surfaces. It is probably in a large measure this that hides much of the crudity of old work.

On the other hand, the surfaces of the walnut cabinet are flat

Fig. 2 Cupboard with typical Jacobean construction. Note that the whole thing is made up of a framework with recessed panels fitting in grooves. The construction is obvious, no attempt being made to conceal it. Compare with the veneered example in **Fig. 3**. About 1650.

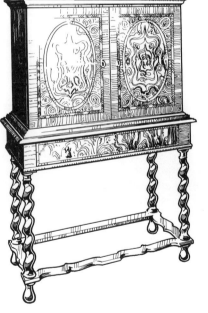

Fig. 3 William and Mary cabinet in walnut. Here the construction is concealed. The banding around the doors for instance has no connection with any framing, but is simply a cross-banding of veneer. Late 17th century.

everywhere, and the grain of the wood is used to produce the decorative appearance. If the wood were plain slabs of timber the effect would be entirely gone. As it is, the cross-banded edges with the herring-bone strip inside and the centre ovals, although quite flat, produce a rich pattern quite as effective in its way as that of the oak piece. The examples of detailed parts in Fig. 4 help to clarify the point.

Fig. 4 Comparison between the two systems of construction, oak and veneered walnut. **A** oak framed-up carcase; **B** veneered walnut carcase; **C** framed-up oak door; **D** flat walnut veneered door; **E** oak drawer fronts; **F** veneered walnut drawer front; **G** oak moulding worked in the solid; **H** cross-grained moulding in walnut cabinet.

Fig. 5 (left) Charles II chair with crown emblem carved in back and stretcher. There is a definite tendency to a lighter form of construction in this chair as compared with earlier examples in **Fig. 5**, page 53. Note too how much finer is the section of the scrolled arms than the square form in **Fig. 3**, page 51. Here construction dictates the general form (note the obvious arrangement of rails in the back). About 1660–1670.

Fig. 6 (right) William and Mary tall-back chair. This is the first example in this book of a chair with back legs splayed backwards. Construction was adapted to suit design. For instance, in the back, it is difficult to tell where the rails join the uprights. About 1690.

The illustrations show how the introduction of veneering altered fundamentally the entire decorative effect of furniture. In the oak, A, C, E, and G, the construction is made use of in the decorative treatment. Note the arrangement of the panelling in C, how it breaks up the surface into three, the panels being recessed and the framework moulded. The whole effect depends upon the varying levels of the surfaces. In the drawers at E, in the one case a moulding gives the appearance of a recessed panel, and in the other the surface is boldly carved in. At G the moulding is worked in the solid.

Taking the veneered walnut examples, B, D, F, and H, the surfaces are flat, and the effect is produced in much the same way as that of a drawing on paper. The grain of the wood is utilized in a decorative way, and cross-bandings and marquetry designs are introduced for the same purpose (D and F). In the moulding, H, a slip of cross-grained walnut is let in, and the moulding worked in this.

Fig. 7 Chairs showing evidence of the transition. In the left-hand example the germ of the carbriole leg is seen. In the other the coming of the splat back of walnut times is heralded. Late 17th century.

Fig. 8 Walnut day-bed of Charles II time. The fact that day beds were in use in Elizabeth's reign is shown by Shakespeare's allusion to them. Early specimens are extremely rare, however, the majority belonging to the restoration period. About 1670.

Fig. 5, 6, and 7 show the gradual evolution taking place in the chair. A note of special interest in the example Fig. 6 is that the back legs are splayed. This is the first example of this feature to be given, chairs up to this time having straight, upright back legs. The day-bed in Fig. 8 is a development of the type mentioned by Shakespeare in *Richard III*.

As a further example of these changes the little table in Fig. 9 is given. This was probably made towards the end of the seventeenth century, and the interesting feature about it is that the maker has tried to emulate the new scheme of things but has carried on with the traditional construction. It was most likely the work of a country carpenter who had seen some furniture of the walnut kind but who had had no experience in making it, and had not the materials to use. It is in oak, and the legs, although neatly turned, have the baluster shaping reminiscent of an earlier period. The wide apron rail is shaped similarly to that of typical William and Mary walnut furniture, and has a cocked bead around the

Fig. 9 Small side table with curiously mixed features. Probably of country origin. Although the whole thing is of oak and the legs are typically Jacobean, there are features which belong to a later period, for example, the shaped rail with cocked bead edging and the inlay around top and drawer front. About 1700.

edge (another 'walnut' feature), but the joints are all pegged, a thing never done in true walnut work. Then the top and the drawer have an inlaid banding of fruit wood around the edges in imitation of cross-banding (such as that in Fig. 3), but the grain runs lengthwise and it is let into the solid oak.

A piece like this would never have been made by a cabinet maker of any standing in a town, and in that sense it is not typical of its period, but it is interesting not only in exemplifying the changes that were taking place, but also in showing the constant lag that maintained in the country districts compared with towns.

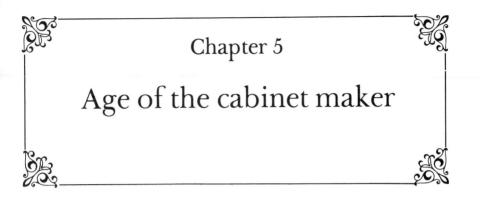

Chapter 5

Age of the cabinet maker

Walnut period

Having seen in the last chapter how new methods of construction enabled a far more refined kind of furniture to be made, we may now turn to the actual pieces that were produced from the Restoration up to the end of Queen Anne's reign in 1714. Perhaps the first thing that strikes one is the multiplicity of types compared with what men had known in the first half of the seventeenth century.

It seems that people had come to have a new outlook on life and were demanding an altogether more luxurious way of living. Perhaps a fair comparison is the way that the average man's point of view has changed since 1913. Not that the results were the same, but the First World War and all that it brought with it set men's minds working along fresh channels. In 1660 it was the Restoration instead of war that prompted the change, and in comparison the changes were even greater.

For one thing there was the reaction from a stern, rigorous form of government to one of licence and laxity. For another there was the strong foreign influence which came as the natural result of the accession of a king who had spent most of his life abroad, soon followed by the reign of a king who actually was a foreigner. The remarkable thing is that the resultant style was not more extravagant than it really was. As it turned out, the walnut period was notable rather for its restraint and dignity, especially in its later stages. The possible reason was that William of Orange did a good deal to check the depraved condition into which the court of Charles II had fallen.

Amongst the pieces that made their first appearance during the walnut period were china cabinets fitted with glass doors, bookcases (also often glazed), writing cabinets, chests of drawers, mirrors, tall clock cases, card tables, and various cabinets elaborately fitted up with small drawers and cupboards. To these may be added chairs with fully upholstered seats and backs. These introductions in themselves reflect the altered conditions, and show that people were no longer content with things which had to answer several purposes. Consider how in earlier days the chest had

Fig. 1 Panelled room from Clifford's Inn. (Now in the Victoria and Albert Museum, South Kensington.) This gives a good idea of the sort of room in which furniture of the Restoration period was placed. About 1686.

served as a seat, table, and travelling chest; or the dining table for every possible purpose for which a table could be needed. By the end of the seventeenth century people indulged in the luxury of collecting china, hence the cabinets for the purpose; they spent their leisure in playing cards and so needed card tables; books were more plentiful, making bookcases essential; and they required not one chair and a few stools in a room, but a full set so that everyone could be comfortable.

Chest of drawers

We saw in chapter 3 how the chest developed into the chest of drawers, and it is interesting to make a comparison between the Jacobean type in Fig. 22, page 62, and the Charles II example in Fig. 2. In date there are not many years' difference between them, but whereas the former is entirely in oak and is made in the old traditional way, the other is of veneered walnut with a flat stretcher and legs of a kind that are not only entirely new in form, but involve a fresh form of construction. From the constructional point of view it is certainly not an advancement upon

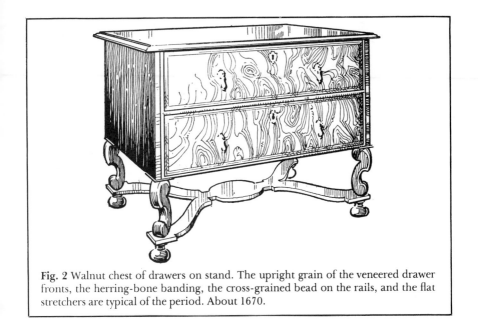

Fig. 2 Walnut chest of drawers on stand. The upright grain of the veneered drawer fronts, the herring-bone banding, the cross-grained bead on the rails, and the flat stretchers are typical of the period. About 1670.

traditional methods in which the stretcher rails would be strongly tenoned into the legs. As it is, the shaped legs have a hole bored at each end, the top one holding a dowel which passes into the bottom of the chest, and the other taking the projecting dowel of the foot, the stretcher fitting between. It is worth taking particular note of this flat stretcher with the foot beneath because it became very popular in the late years of the seventeenth century.

A glance at the chest itself shows that in construction and form it bears out the changes dealt with more fully in the last chapter. The drawer fronts are flat, and around the edges is a herring-bone banding, a typical 'walnut' feature. One special note of interest is that along the drawer rails and front edges of the ends is a flat half-round moulding with the grain running crosswise. Charles II and William and Mary work often had this feature. Later it declined, its place being taken by a cocked bead fixed around the edges of the drawer fronts. The latter was really a more practical idea because the bead helped to protect the edges of the veneer, preventing the latter from being chipped away.

Cross-grained mouldings Mention of the cross-grained bead brings us to another feature which was used almost exclusively in walnut work, the cross-grained moulding. It will be appreciated that to make a solid cross-grained moulding would not be practical. It would have no strength, be liable to twist, and would certainly shrink. The plan was therefore adopted of applying a thin strip of cross-grained wood to a solid groundwork, the grain of which ran lengthwise. The groundwork provided the strength and the thinness of the layer had sufficient 'give' to overcome the shrinkage difficulty.

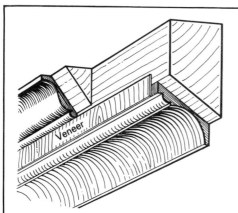

Fig. 3 How cross-graned walnut mouldings were built up. Strips of cross-grained walnut are glued to a groundwork of pine or oak.

Fig. 4 William and Mary chest of drawers on stand. The inverted cup turned legs and flat stretcher were extremely popular at the period. The round frieze continued into the Queen Anne period. Late 17th century.

If the moulding were extra big the work would be allowed to stand until full shrinkage had taken place, when the inevitable splits would be filled in. All but the smallest mouldings were made in this way, and even these in the best work were cross-grained. It is a point to look for in an old piece. Fig. 3 shows how a cornice moulding was built up, and the illustration on page 111 gives a number of sections, in some of which the facing layer of walnut is also shown.

A rather later chest, dating from about 1690, is given in Fig. 4, and it will be noticed that, although it embodies many similar features to the chest in Fig. 2, it is of altogether better proportions and approaches a period when walnut furniture was at its best. The drawer fronts are

Fig. 5 William and Mary and Queen Anne chests of drawers. Late 17th and early 18th century respectively.

veneered and have the herring-bone banding around the edges, and there is the half-round moulding on the drawer rails and cabinet ends. The frieze of flat rounded section veneered with cross-grained walnut should be noted because a great deal of walnut furniture had this detail. It was copied from the cornice and frieze built in many houses of the period. Turned legs with the inverted cup shape are peculiar to William and Mary pieces, and, although other shapes were used, they are usually a good indication of the period. Note that the flat stretcher similar to that in Fig. 2 is still used.

One other point to note is that the veneering has the effect of hiding the construction almost entirely. Take the stand, for instance. There is no indication of where the rails are joined to the legs. This is in contrast with the older oak furniture in which all the joints were apparent, and in which the grain always ran in the direction which strength demanded. The appreciation of points such as this enables one to understand the root of the changes that were taking place.

Tallboys   Two other chests are given in Fig. 5. That to the left is late seventeenth century, but the other is of Queen Anne's reign and shows the final development of the walnut period. It is a close approach to that delightful looking, but rather impractical article the tallboy chest. Presumably men felt that the drawer was so extremely useful (and it undoubtedly was) that the more they could fit into a piece the more useful it became. It was like many another good idea, spoilt by being taken to extremes. Any reader who has possessed one of these tallboys will appreciate the nuisance of having to mount up on a chair to reach the contents of the top drawers.

In this chest we also have a feature which we shall frequently run across in Queen Anne work, the apron piece. This is the shaped rail joining the legs beneath the lower drawers. It appears in the chest in Fig. 4, and in Fig. 5. It was the natural result of the introduction of veneering or, to be more accurate, it was a detail which was made possible only by veneering. If, for instance, the veneer were stripped off, the joints of the various rails would be exposed with the applied apron piece showing beneath. Such an arrangement would be unsightly, but when covered with veneer makes an attractive and characteristic feature. Sometimes the shaped edges were covered with a cocked bead. The chest in Fig. 4 has this detail.

One other outstanding feature of the right-hand chest, Fig. 5, is that in it we have the first introduction to the cabriole leg which enjoyed so vast a popularity in the eighteenth century. This will be dealt with more fully presently when we come to speak about chairs, but it is worth-while noting its use in pieces of this kind.

Drawer construction   In all these chests, the drawer sides, backs, and bottoms were invariably of oak. Walnut was still a comparatively rare wood – it was probably not planted in this country until Elizabeth's reign – and on that account was costly. Furthermore oak was the better

Fig. 6 Double-domed writing cabinet veneered with walnut. A particularly fine piece of cabinet-work. Note that the domed cornice is repeated at the sides. About 1700. Photograph by courtesy of Mallet and Son (Antiques) Ltd., London.

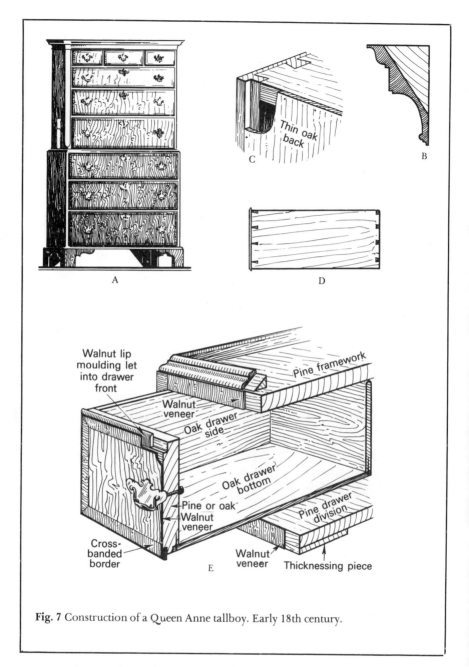

Fig. 7 Construction of a Queen Anne tallboy. Early 18th century.

calculated to withstand the wear inevitable on the sliding surfaces. The grain of the bottom invariably ran from front to back as in Fig. 7 and since it was rigidly fixed in rebates in the drawer sides, it was bound to split owing to shrinkage. At a later period the grain ran from side to side and, since it was held in grooves without glue, it was free to shrink without splitting.

Fig. 8 Walnut cabinet on chest-of-drawers. All the mouldings are cross-grained, a typical feature of the period. About 1710. Courtesy of W.R. Harvey and Co. (Antiques) Ltd.

Oak was also used for the groundwork of the drawer fronts, though there was a tendency to use pine for the purpose, because experience showed that oak did not grip the glue as well as pine. Also, the figure in the oak was liable to show through the veneer eventually because of the shrinkage of the softer parts of the timber. However, it is no criterion, for both were used for the purpose.

When a walnut moulding was required at the edges (except in the case of the cocked bead) a slip of cross-grained walnut was first let in all round and the veneer laid over this. This enabled the moulding to be worked in the walnut at the edges, see Fig. 7. It was unnecessary in a cocked bead, for this could be applied afterwards in a rebate worked for the purpose.

Chairs and stools

The chair as we left it in our chapter on Jacobean work was still a sturdily built piece of work though tending to become lighter. A few were made with stuffed seats, and occasionally upholstered backs were added, but for the most part they were entirely of wood – or possibly were fitted with a leather seat stretched over the rails. This, though being softer than wood, could hardly be called upholstery.

After the middle of the century there arose a custom of using cane for the better type of chair back, and rushes for the commoner type. Upholstery, too, was used, though this did not become really popular until the reign of William and Mary. I may mention here that springs were never used. As a matter of passing interest, it was not until the nineteenth century that these came into use.

Twist turning Caning is usually associated with the tall-back chairs which became popular during the second half of the seventeenth century, and this brings us to an interesting development, that of twist turning. Until about 1625 or so only plain, straightforward turning had been attempted. The work was mounted in a curious contrivance known as the pole lathe, over which a long springy pole (hence the name) was suspended from a bracket in the wall. To the end of the pole was fixed a rope which stretched down to a drum attached to the chuck or around the work itself. It was taken a turn around this and then down to a treadle. Thus when the operator depressed the treadle the work was revolved in a forward motion and the pole above was bent downwards. When the pressure on the treadle was released the pole sprang back, turning the work in the opposite direction.

It is obvious from this that the actual cutting could be done whilst the work was revolving forwards only, and when one considers the toughness of English oak, and the large size in which many of the old bulbous turnings were made, it is not surprising that the turners did not go in for a great deal for experiment. However, some ingenious craftsman, probably noticing the spiral made by his gouge as he pased it rapidly along the surface, did try his hand at forming a spiral or twist, and by a combination of preliminary sawing out, rough turning, and use of carving tools to finish off, produced a form of twist.

The wood was first turned to cylindrical form, the twist marked out by wrapping a piece of card or something similar spiralwise along it, and the shaping formed by carving with a gouge, and finished off with rasp or

Fig. 9 Tall-back chair with upholstered seat. Note that the top back rail is simply pegged to the turned uprights. The legs which are suggestive of the cabriole shape are in reality a series of scrolls. Late 17th century.

file, then scraped. There may be a few of these old pole lathes in use in the outlying districts of Buckinghamshire, where turnings for chairs are still made on a large scale.

A chair with twist turnings was given in Fig. 5 on page 74, and in this we see the passing out of the old oak tradition. Chair making suffered something of a decline in the third quarter of the seventeenth century, at any rate from the point of view of construction. Instead of the seat rails being strongly tenoned between the legs, they were merely placed on top with no stronger attachment than a dowel turned at the top of the legs. The same thing applied to the top rail of the back, which was simply fitted to dowels at the ends of the uprights. This detail is shown clearly in the chair in Fig. 9, though in this case the front seat rail is still tenoned between the legs.

This chair is fairly typical of the tall-back which persisted until the end of the seventeenth century. Turning was used considerably, even for the tops of the shaped front legs, and it is interesting to note that the back legs splay backwards. Even many of the early tall-backs did not have this detail, and if ever it were essentail in any chair it was in one which was essentially lightly built and had a high back. For someone to lean back even slightly would be dangerous.

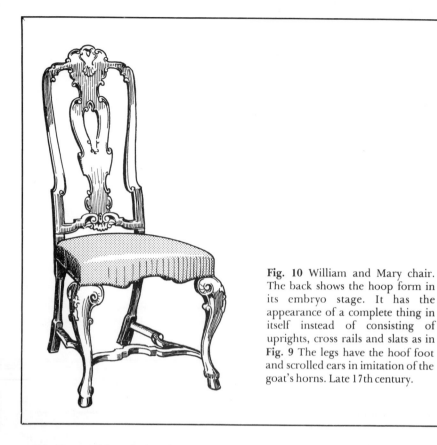

Fig. 10 William and Mary chair. The back shows the hoop form in its embryo stage. It has the appearance of a complete thing in itself instead of consisting of uprights, cross rails and slats as in **Fig. 9** The legs have the hoof foot and scrolled ears in imitation of the goat's horns. Late 17th century.

The legs of the chair, Fig. 9, are interesting in that they foreshadow the cabriole leg which was shortly to become popular, though when examined closely it is seen that they consist actually of a number of scrolls joined together with floral and leaf carving. Scroll work of this kind was used widely in chairs and stands of all kinds. It is seen in the front stretcher rail and in the back of that in Fig. 9.

Chairs with cabriole legs   The introduction of the cabriole leg seemed to strike a new note in the design of chairs. It was not simply that a new *motif* was being used, but that the whole conception of the design became altered. Compare, for example, the two chairs Fig. 9 and 10. It is obvious that the one has turned uprights whilst the other has shaped ones, but, in addition, there is an entirely new spirit in that in Fig. 10. In the earlier example, Fig. 9, one is conscious of a series of parts jointed together in an obvious sort of way. It is not suggested that this is a fault, but simply that the construction is at once apparent. One can count up the parts – two uprights, cresting rail, lower rail, seat rail, stretcher, and so on. And the earlier the chair the more obvious the parts and their purpose becomes.

Now turn to Fig. 10. It is not easy to see where the uprights and the top rail of the back begin and end. They merge one into the other, and the same thing applies to the slat and the rail beneath. The back is one whole, so to speak, and we shall find that this feeling becomes still more apparent in later chairs.

Reverting to the legs again, these are an early form of the cabriole type, and exemplify the Dutch influence which the accession of William of Orange brought with it. The probability is that many of these chairs were the work of foreign craftsmen who settled down here. A cabriole leg is by no means an easy thing to make, and it is doubtful whether a native craftsman could have turned out a really fine shape without previous experience. The awkward point about making the leg is that it is difficult to set down the true shape on paper. It can be drawn at the front, side, and possibly three-quarter positions, but the actual leg is seen from all angles and is normally viewed from above, a viewpoint which the drawing does not present.

Furthermore, in the very nature of the work the guiding lines on the wood are cut away as the work proceeds, because the whole thing is more or less rounded in section. In actual practice the leg is cut out of a square right through to the over-all shape when looked at from the front. A corresponding shape is cut at the side, this producing a square-cut shape. The point to realize is that the cutting of the first shape automatically removes the lines of the second shape, and it is only by temporarily replacing the sawn-away parts that the shape can be cut true. In any case the resulting shape has only a distant resemblance to the finished line, and it is in the final shaping that experience is needed, because there are no square lines to which to work. Everything is curved in both directions and it is only by eye that a really fine shape can be produced, one which looks well when seen from every angle. The whole thing is complicated when carving is to appear, because sufficient thickness has to be allowed for this, and the presence of these plain lumps is apt to give a false impression of the shape as a whole.

We have gone into these practical points at some length because the cabriole leg became so characteristic a feature of furniture for the following seventy-five years or so. Really fine legs are few and far between, the majority being overdone in the shape, and we shall find that they deteriorated considerably after Queen Anne's reign until rescued by the school of Chippendale.

In the present instance, Fig. 10, it will be noticed that the legs terminate in a hoof foot, whilst at the top the sides are scrolled in imitation of the horns of the goat. These details are often found in William and Mary furniture, after which they gave place to the turned club foot, as illustrated in Fig. 11. In the meantime it should be noted that the legs are still linked together with stretcher rails. It is true that the last-named are on an altogether lighter scale than in earlier pieces (see Fig. 5, page 53) and are gracefully shaped, but the chair-maker has not yet felt confident enough to omit them entirely, which was the next stage in the development of the chair.

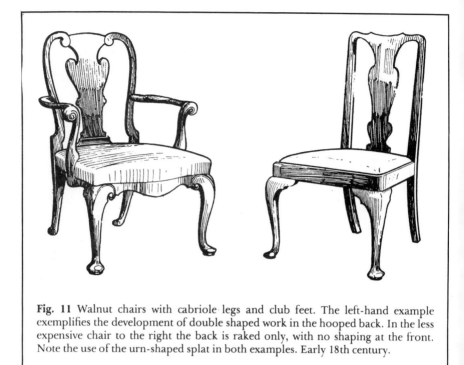

Fig. 11 Walnut chairs with cabriole legs and club feet. The left-hand example exemplifies the development of double shaped work in the hooped back. In the less expensive chair to the right the back is raked only, with no shaping at the front. Note the use of the urn-shaped splat in both examples. Early 18th century.

Another feature of the chair in Fig. 10 met with for the first time is the curve in the rake of the back, and it is interesting to glance at the diagram in Fig. 12, which shows the various stages of development. There is the earliest straight post J cut from a square of timber and continuing from leg to back in a straight line. This was used mostly in the old settles of Gothic times (see Fig. 18, page 31). Then came the idea of setting the back at an angle K, a phase which lasted until past the middle of the seventeenth century. An example is given in Fig. 2, page 49. In the same period in a few chairs little blocks were added at the bottom as at L to help to counterbalance the weight. This is exemplified in Fig 20, page 33. Next, the legs were at last splayed as at M, though the back still remained straight without any curve (see Fig. 6, page 74). N gives the next development, as in the chair in Fig. 10, whilst O shows the shape which the majority of chairs in the later eighteenth century had, of which Fig. 2, page 116 is an example.

A last point to note about the chair in Fig. 10 is the shaped splat. This was something quite fresh (see last example in Fig. 9), and had certain definite stages in development. It is shown in the armchair in Fig. 11 in its most characteristic form. Apart from its shaped edges it follows the general line of the back when viewed from the side.

These two chairs in Fig. 11 exemplify the walnut period in its fullest stage of development in the Queen Anne period. That to the left is especially characteristic in the shape of the back, the splat, and the full

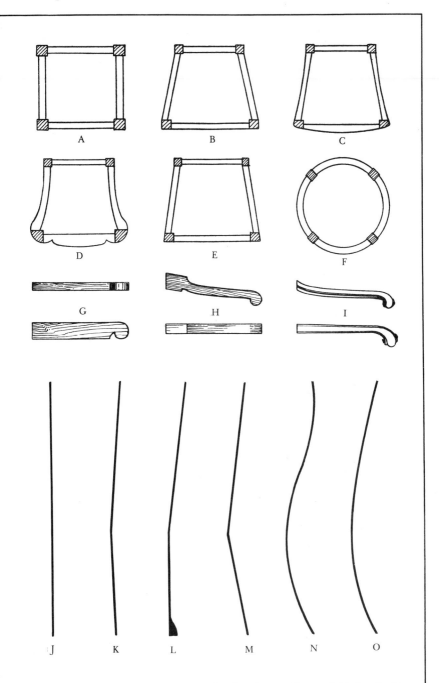

Fig. 12 Details of chairs during the periods. Plan shapes of seats: **A** Tudor Gothic; **B** Jacobean; **C** and **D** walnut; **E** mid 18th century; **F** late 18th century. Arms: **G** Tudor Gothic; **H** Jacobean; **I** early walnut period. Shapes of backs: **J**, **K** and **L** Tudor Gothic; **M** early walnut; **N** late walnut; **O** second half 18th century.

cabriole legs with turned club feet. Note that the back is appreciably lower and that the shaping of the uprights has become more pronounced, especially in the rounded shape at the top. The splat, too, is entirely solid and has an urn-like formation.

The fact that the backs were shaped in both front and side elevations made them extremely expensive to produce, and it was for this reason that the square back type to the right in Fig. 11 was made for a more economical job. The uprights merely taper and they are quite straight in their rake. In the best chairs, however, the full shaping was given, and on some models the back was entirely veneered with cross-grain walnut. Another feature to note is the complete absence of stretcher rails.

Just as the development in the shape of the rake of the back can be followed in a series of stages, so the plain shape of the seats developed on certain characteristic lines. These are shown diagrammatically in Fig. 12, from the square box-like formation of early Tudor times to the tapering shape of the Elizabethan and Jacobean periods, and the elaborately shaped seats of walnut furniture. Later on there was a return to the simpler form.

One other innovation in the walnut period in connection with the seats was the loose drop-in variety shown in Fig. 11 to the right. These were not used exclusively, the 'stuff-over' method (left in Fig. 11) being also used frequently.

The development of upholstery has already been mentioned, and in Fig. 13 we have the fully upholstered armchair of about 1705. The projecting wings and the scrolled arms are especially characteristic, and bear out the prevailing popularity of shaped work.

Stools The two stools in Fig. 14 are of the William and Mary (left) and Queen Anne (right) periods. In the earlier specimens the legs are actually turned, and the scrolled and recessed detail is carved out of the shape. The shaped stretchers are similar to those already shown in the chest of drawers in Fig. 2, except that the edges are moulded instead of being square. In the Queen Anne stool the stretchers are omitted. The legs are worth noting in that they terminate with spade feet. These are carved out entirely, no turning being used. Other features often found are the shell carving on the knee with the pendant husks below, and the scrolls at the sides immediately beneath the ears.

The day-bed in the form shown in Fig. 8, page 75, did not last into the eighteenth century. Its place was taken by the settee, which was rather like two or more chairs joined together side by side. There was sometimes a centre leg, though it was frequently omitted.

Furniture for writing

Until the time of the Civil War the average man attempted little in the way of writing. The vast majority of people could not write at all, and

Fig. 13 Upholstered armchair. Although thickly padded, these chairs were never fitted with springs. Early 18th century.

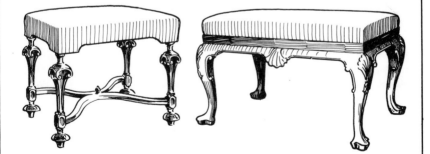

Fig. 14 Stools of the walnut period. The legs of the left-hand stool are turned and the carving is cut into the turning. Late 17th century. Note the omission of the stretcher in the right-hand stool. The shell and husk carving is typical. Early 18th century.

those who could did all their writing at their place of business. If they had any writing to do at home it certainly did not occur to them that they needed a special piece of furniture, except possibly a small desk of the Bible box type shown in Fig. 18, page 60. It was the time of the professional letter writer, that curious semi-educated individual who would write a letter on any subject for anyone who would care to pay the fee.

The changing habits of people after the Restoration gave considerable impetus to the art of writing. Education was spreading and the vast commercial developments abroad encouraged at least an elementary education, since it offered employment to men who could read and write. Furthermore, with the development of business there arose a new class which could afford to spend money on furnishing. This was the merchant class, whose way of life made writing essential, and men of this type probably found it necessary to have a piece of furniture in their homes at which they could write. Remember that most merchants lived at their places of business in those days.

Furthermore, it was a period when literature was growing rapidly. Pepys, in his diary, speaks of the books he collects, and early in the eighteenth century the *Spectator* was started, a publication in which essays and letters by various well-known men appeared. This in itself encouraged people to read and, in turn, came the prompting for men to write letters themselves. In short, it was an age when more and more people began to write, and it is therefore not surprising to find that cabinets specially intended for writing were first made at this time.

The bureau Furniture for writing was made in three forms, the bureau, the secretaire, and the writing table. The form of the bureau seems to suggest that it was evolved from the Bible box or reading desk of Jacobean times, except that the lid or fall was given a greater angle, and was made so that it opened out the opposite way to give a suitable space for writing. Turn for a moment to Fig. 18C, page 60 and compare it with the left-hand bureau in Fig. 15. If allowance is made for the difference in style the likeness is really remarkable. The bureau is of the William and Mary period, and it virtually is just a 'Bible box' on a stand fitted with drawers. The interior is fitted up for stationery and the fall rests upon lopers when opened, but in general form it is similar to the oak piece.

It is interesting to note that there are many features in this bureau which we have already run across in other pieces. There are, firstly, the 'inverted cup' turned legs, joined at the bottom by flat stretcher rails. Both these details appeared in the chest in Fig. 4. Then there is the apron piece and the use throughout of cross-grained mouldings. Points like this go to show how fashion had spread to all kinds of furniture.

It must soon have become apparent that a small bureau on a stand of this type, while suitable for a man who might write one letter or so in a week, was not of much use to the man who required to settle down seriously to any extent of writing. For one thing, it was not large enough;

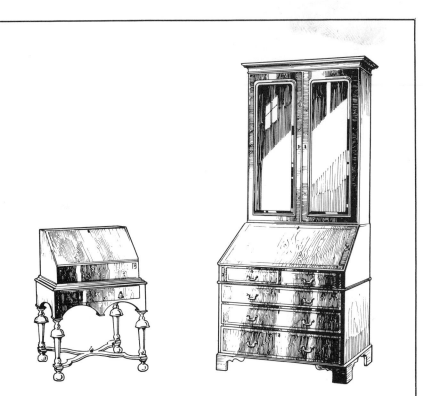

Fig. 15 Small bureau and bureau with cupboard. The inverted cup shape of the turned legs in the small bureau shows the William and Mary period. Late 17th century. The mirrored doors of the cupboard on the right were a common feature in Queen Anne pieces of this kind. Early 18th century.

Fig. 17 Small walnut writing table. This exemplifies well the way in which the construction was entirely concealed by the use of veneer. The apron piece beneath the drawers is often seen in Queen Anne tables. Early 18th century.

for another, its accommodation was far too limited. So came into being the full size bureau, in which the whole of the lower portion was taken up with drawers, and which was deep enough to enable a bookcase to be erected above. An example is given to the right in Fig. 15. Note that even here convention still influences the general construction, for the bureau is made in two parts which separate beneath the top drawer in the same way that the bureau to the left separates at the stand. In later bureaux the sides were made in a single piece each.

A detail in this bureau appearing for the first time are the bracket feet, as they are termed. They continued in one variation or another for the whole of the eighteenth centry. Another innovation is the mirrors in the doors of the bookcase. Mirrors were still something of a novelty even in the late seventeenth century. They had been invented by the Venetians as early as the fourteenth century but, although a few were made here by Italian craftsmen in the beginning of the seventeenth century, it was not until the last quarter of the century that they were made in any quantity. Even so they could only be made in small sizes. Anything larger than the panels of the bookcase in Fig. 15 would be extremely uncommon. When larger ones were needed it was customary to join two or more sections together and cover the joints with a bead. The edges were usually bevelled and often a star device was cut in the surface to give a touch of decoration.

In many bookcases of the kind wood panels were fitted, and the interior was fitted up either with plain shelves for books or with a series of small drawers, pigeon holes, and cupboards. Sometimes, too, the cornice moulding was carried up in a series of curves, the top rails of the door following the general shape. The china cabinet in Fig. 22 is a fairly typical design showing these features.

Writing tables   The second piece used entirely for writing was the table of which Fig. 17 is an example. Note here the presence of the apron piece seen in previous pieces, and the cabriole legs. Other tables followed the same idea already noted in the case of the bureau, the legs being omitted and the entire lower part filled in with drawers and a cupboard. The latter was usually recessed to allow comfortable space for the knees.

The secretaire   A secretaire is given in Fig. 19. The whole of the front of the upper part is pivoted at the bottom so that it drops down to a horizontal position, thus forming a large writing top. The interior was usually elaborately fitted up with pigeon-holes, drawers and cupboards. It will be seen that the frieze is bowed as in previous specimens and that the moulding is cross-grained. Another feature frequently found in work of the period is the wide cross-banding and small herring-bone banding around the fall front. In this particular case the corners are mitred, but they are often found with the corners butted, the upright bandings running right through and the horizontal pieces contained between them.

Fig. 16 Walnut cabinet with seaweed marquetry. The convex frieze is a typical feature; in this case it forms a drawer front. Queen Anne period. Photograph by courtesy of the Victoria & Albert Museum, London.

Fig. 18 Detail of a cabinet heading veneered with walnut and with gilt gesso mouldings and detail. Queen Anne period. Photograph by courtesy of Mallet and Son (Antiques) Ltd., London.

Figure 20 Walnut bureau-bookcase, early eighteenth century. Photograph by courtesy of the Victoria & Albert Museum, London.

The veneer is in four pieces, arranged in quartered form. It will be realized that it would be almost impossible to obtain so large a sheet of veneer in a single piece, hence the necessity for jointing. The craftsman, realizing this, hit upon the remarkably successful method of jointing it up in quarters as shown, so taking advantage of necessity to obtain a decorative effect. The four pieces of veneer would be cut next to each other from the same piece of timber so that the grain would be practically identical. It was merely necessary to reverse two of them to obtain a perfectly balanced whole.

Coming now to the lower carcase, the bracket feet are of a slightly different design from those in Fig. 15, and the drawer rails have the flat bead along their faces. Sometimes a double bead was used instead of the single one.

It is often found in these old secretaires that the fall front has split badly along its length, and this is due to the construction. The groundwork was clamped, that is, the grain of the main panel ran horizontally, and at the ends were clamps, the grain of which ran from top to bottom. A certain amount of shrinkage was inevitable, and as the clamps were glued on the panel had to split. Any blemish of this kind inevitably shows through to the veneer, with the result that this also splits. It was the early days of veneering and the craftsmen had yet to experience the difficulties that the process entailed.

On small work there was no difficulty – in fact on any work in which clamping was unnecessary the work was fairly straightforward. For instance, on cabinet sides the top and bottom provided the strength across the grain, and as the latter ran in the same direction in all parts there was no harm done in the event of shrinkage. It was only on such work as this fall front, where there was nothing to give support across the grain, that clamping was necessary, with the consequent attendant risk of splitting.

China cabinets

It was probably Queen Mary who set the fashion for collecting china. Trade with the East brought about the importation of Chinese pottery and it soon became a popular craze for people of wealth to collect fine specimens. Cabinets to contain them followed as a matter of course, and it was, therefore, in the last quarter of the seventeenth century that the first china cabinets were made. An example is given in Fig. 22. There are many typical features about it; the turned legs with the inverted cup detail, the apron piece finished at the edge with a cross-grained bead, the flat stretcher rails, the cross-banded doors, and the shaped cornice, also cross-grained. Glazed doors were essential, and in them we have an early example of the barred door.

The probability is that in the first instance the bars were not purely decorative. Panes of glass in a large size were difficult to produce, and the

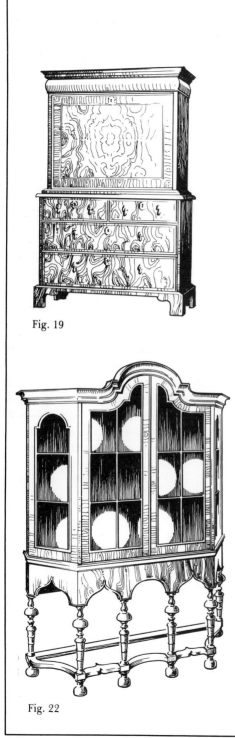

Fig. 19

Fig. 21

Fig. 19 Queen Anne period secretaire. The front of the upper carcase is hinged so that it drops down and forms a writing top. The inside is fitted up for stationery. Early 18th century.

Figure 21 Walnut veneered china cabinet. The barred doors owed their origin to the difficulty of producing glass in large panes. They were cross-grained with a rib at the back. Early 18th century.

Fig. 22 China cabinet with barred doors on stand. The craze for collecting china, encouraged by Queen Mary, was the cause of the introduction of the cina cabinet. Late 17th century.

Fig. 22

method of subdividing up the space with bars to enable small panes to be used suggested itself as a solution to the difficulty. In the event it proved extremely successful as a form of decorative treatment; so much so that during the eighteenth century bars were used in various designs almost as a matter of course. It is just another example of the way in which advantage can be taken of the limitations of material to produce an effect which not only looks well but seems characteristic of the work.

Mirrors

Whilst on the subject of glasswork, we may turn to the mirror, which was first made in fairly large quantities towards the end of the seventeenth century. Earlier examples are in existence, but they were mostly made in Italy and imported, though a few Italian craftsmen settled in the country early in the seventeenth century and began producing in a small way. The chief impetus came later, when works were established by the Duke of Buckingham in London. Mention of them is made by Evelyn in his diary of 1676, when he paid a visit to them.

Two examples of hanging wall mirrors are given in Fig. 23 and 25. That to the left is perhaps the more usual type. The actual framework is a rather flat moulding with the grain running crosswise. Typical sections of the mouldings used are given in Fig. 36. They were built up on a

Fig. 23   Fig. 25

Fig. 23 Simple mirror. The shaped boards at head and foot were invariably used in these plain mirrors. Early 18th century.

Fig. 25 Partly gilt mirror. This shows the strong architectural influence sometimes found in Queen Anne mirrors. Early 18th century.

Fig. 24 Mahogany mirror with all the characteristics of the walnut period. Photograph by courtesy of the Victoria and Albert Museum, London.

foundation of pine or oak to provide the strength, and the walnut was glued to the upper face in cross-grained strips. The section was then worked as in an ordinary moulding. Usually the top corners were either rounded, as in Fig. 23, or they had the rather typical series of short squares and curves, such as in the door in Fig. 21. The fretted pieces at top and bottom are invariably found in such mirrors.

The mirror in Fig. 24, although it is mahogany and dates from about 1730, has typical features of the walnut period. The other example, Fig. 25, is of quite different feeling, having an architectural character probably inspired by the details found in the windows and doorways of the period. The groundwork is in walnut and the carved mouldings and details are gilt. Both types were produced in fairly large quantities, and the size was invariably small for the reason already given. In addition, small toilet glasses were made, these having either a plain stand with uprights between which the mirror was pivoted, or a small nest of drawers to hold cosmetics arranged with the uprights tenoned in above.

Clock cases

Up to the present we have not dealt with clocks, for the good reason that nothing in the way of a clock case was made before the second half of the seventeenth century. Earlier clocks were of what is known as the lantern type, consisting of a brass framework with turned corner pillars and a round dial fixed at the front. Of the movements of clocks there is no space to deal in this book. It would require a book in itself to explain the various kinds and the phases through which the mechanism passed. Suffice it to say that the early type were fitted with the verge movement in which the teeth of a rotating crown wheel engaged the pallets of a balance arbor. The pendulum came into use soon after the middle of the seventeenth century.

A lantern clock is shown in Fig. 27. It was intended to stand on a bracket, the power being supplied by a weight suspended by a chain. A single hour hand was fitted, pointing to numerals engraved on either a brass or silvered dial. A striking mechanism was usually fitted, the bell being mounted upon curved metal bars as in the present example. Just below it a fretted brass pediment was fitted, this being generally of the dolphin device and engraved as shown. At the corners turned brass finials were fitted.

Bracket clocks During the second half of the seventeenth century wooden bracket clock cases became popular, and these were generally of the form shown in Fig. 28. They were roughly square in shape and a 'basket' top was fitted to provide interior space for the bell. Various kinds were made, some being of walnut, cross-grained as in the general run of contemporary furniture, others were veneered with tortoiseshell, elaborate marquetry (this form of decoration is dealt with later), and

Fig. 26 Grandfather clock case entirely of walnut veneered upon oak. All mouldings are cross-grained. Early 18th century.

Four stages in bracket clocks from Jacobean times until the late 18th century.

Fig. 27 Brass lantern clock. This type was made to stand upon a bracket, power being supplied by a weight suspended upon a chain. First half 17th century.

Fig. 28 Walnut bracket clock. This is the type known as the basket top, this being introduced to give space for the bell. About 1700.

Fig. 29 Bell top bracket clock in ebony. Note the use of the arched door to allow space for the upper dial. About 1740.

Fig. 30 Domed top mahogany clock case. Clocks of this kind usually had white dials with black markings. Second half 18th century.

Fig. 27

Fig. 28

Fig. 26

Fig. 29

Fig. 30

some were in ebony. In some the basket top was of brass fretted and engraved, the better to allow the sound of the bell to emerge. In most the cases were glazed on all four sides to allow the mechanism to be seen.

Later, during the first half of the eighteenth century, the 'bell-top' clock was introduced, the name arising out of the formation of the top. One example is given in Fig. 29. In this the square front has been heightened and the top of the door is rounded to give space to the small dial which records either the date or enables the clock to be set either to 'strike' or 'silent'. It should be noted that no bracket clocks of this type were fitted with a seconds hand because a movement of this kind needs a far longer pendulum than could be accommodated in a small case. The fourth clock Fig. 30, belongs to an altogether later period, the second half of the eighteenth century, but it is given here so that easy comparison of the styles can be made.

Grandfather clocks   Speaking of the long pendulum brings us to the grandfather case introduced during the reign of Charles II. The details in them were similar to those in the furniture of the time, though there was something characteristic in their treatment which seems to belong peculiarly to clock cases. They were mostly of veneered walnut and occasionally ebony, and the hoods were made to slide either forwards or upwards, usually the former. They were generally flat at the top, as in the example in Fig. 26, and twist columns were fitted at the corners, these opening with the door. In many specimens a piece of bottle glass was introduced in the large door in the waist to enable the movement of the pendulum to be seen. This was fitted in either a round or oval frame.

Frets were often introduced in the frieze, these being backed with silk, and the mouldings were of a delicate type, far finer than those usually used in furniture. The workmanship was invariably of a high quality, and this, coupled with the characteristic details, suggests that it became customary for some men to specialize in case making as distinct from the ordinary cabinet making. The late seventeenth century examples were usually veneered with marquetry, whilst the Queen Anne specimens were of plain walnut, decorated with cross-bandings and herring-bone bandings.

Marquetry

We have had occasion to refer to this form of decoration, and we may here conveniently explain what this was. We saw in Elizabethan and Jacobean work that inlay was used considerably as decoration. This consisted of recessing out a solid background to a depth of 3 mm. ($\frac{1}{8}$ in.) or more and inserting pieces of wood of a different kind from that of the background. The whole point about it was that it was cut in the solid and that the recesses had to be chopped out with chisel and gouge. With solid work there was no other alternative.

We saw also that a new method of treatment was introduced in the form of veneering, and the coming of this enabled an entirely new method of 'inlaying' to be used. In this the inlaying was done in the veneer before being laid and, although this at first may not seem to carry with it any special advantage, it did in reality make a tremendous difference, involving an entirely new technique. The reason for this was that the veneer, being thin, could be cut out with a saw instead of having to be laboriously chopped away with the chisel. A comparison is that of fretwork. The reader knows what fine sweeping curves can be cut with the fretsaw. But imagine how limited the result would be if all the spaces had to be chopped away with the gouge!

This use of the saw, then, in itself made a tremendous difference in the designs that could be cut, but there was more in it than this. By fixing together two sheets of veneer of different kinds of wood and cutting through them at the same time both would have *exactly* the same design. Thus it was only necessary to separate the sheets and interchange the parts and a perfect fit was obtained.

It was obviously necessary to use an extremely fine saw blade, very like a fretsaw blade. A special sawing bench, known as a 'donkey', was used. The worker sat astride and rested the feet on a treadle connected with a vice above which gripped the veneer. The saw frame was horizontal and was worked with the right hand, whilst the veneer was moved about with the left. When the whole design had been cut it was assembled on a bench, the parts being interchanged as required. Any shading required was done by dipping the parts into hot sand. The whole was then glued to paper face downwards and handed to the cabinet maker for gluing down.

It was first used about 1675, and the early efforts were in comparison crude, consisting for the most part of flowers, leaf and scroll work arranged in a conventional design. A few years of experience, however, made the workers extremely skilful, and they began to produce some extremely elaborate patterns, known usually as seaweed marquetry, in which the detail was very fine. Curiously enough, however, marquetry did not retain its popularity for very long, for in Queen Anne's reign plain walnut was mostly used in which the beauty of the grain, combined with cross-banding, provided the decorative appearance.

Tables

It is a remarkable thing that there do not appear to have been made any large dining tables in the walnut style during the reigns of either William and Mary or Queen Anne. Possibly it was that the cabinet makers found a serious difficulty in veneering such large tops owing to the liability of the groundwork to shrink and split. They never used walnut in the solid except for such parts as legs and turnings. However this may be, one can only draw the conclusion that the old Jacobean table in oak continued to be used, and a strangely inconsistent arrangement it must have seemed.

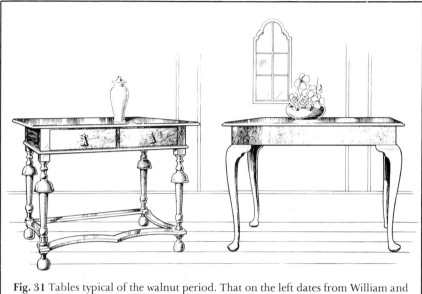

Fig. 31 Tables typical of the walnut period. That on the left dates from William and Mary's reign. Note in particular the inverted cup shape of the turned legs. Late 17th century. The other was made in the time of Queen Anne. The cabriole legs show this. Early 18th century.

Small side tables, card tables, and so on, were made and two examples are given in Fig. 31. That to the left belongs to the William and Mary period (note the inverted cup turned legs and flat stretchers), and the other is a later type made in the early years of the eighteenth century. Card tables were similar in appearance, the top being made double so that it would open out to form an approximately square shape. The two back legs were pivoted so that they could pull out and support the overhanging top. Cards had become an extremely popular form of amusement at the period.

Lacquered furniture

Mention has already been made of the increased trade with the East resulting in the importation of Oriental pottery. Other items imported were lacquered cabinets of entirely Chinese workmanship. These were plain rectangular cupboards with the interior fitted up with small drawers and cupboards. To be of practical use in a Western room they needed mounting upon a stand, and it therefore became the custom to import the cabinets and to make special stands for them which were either gilt or silvered. Fig. 33 is such a cabinet and stand, and shows the elaborate carving with which the stands were invariably decorated. Later it became customary for the lacquered cabinets themselves to be imitated in this country – in fact lacquering became a popular craze for people of

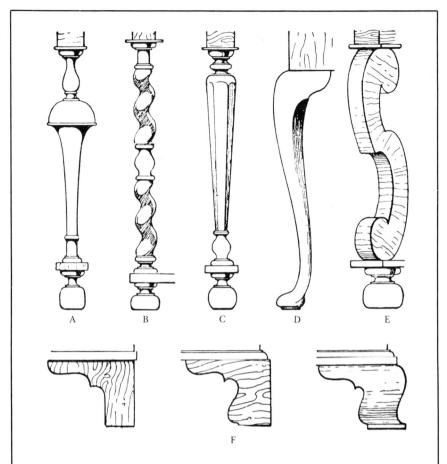

Fig. 32 Typical legs and feet used in the walnut period. **A** inverted cup turning; **B** twist turning; **C** octagonal shape. All these belong to William and Mary period. **D** Queen Anne cabriole leg; **E** double scroll leg of late 17th century; **F** bracket feet.

Fig. 33 Lacquered cabinet on stand. Oriental cabinets were frequently imported, and carved stands were made to hold them. Later rather crude imitations of Oriental lacquer were attempted here. Second half 17th century.

leisure to take up. A *Treatise on japanning and varnishing* was published by Stalker and Parker which purported to explain the whole art of lacquering, but no lacquering was ever produced here which could in the slightest degree compare with the true native oriental work.

The craze for lacquered work quickly spread to other forms of furniture and clock cases, bedsteads, and cabinets of all kinds were made in beech and lacquered in various colours. Red and black were the chief shades. Sometimes existing cabinets which had been finely veneered with walnut were lacquered over to satisfy the fashionable craze.

Fig. 33

Fig. 34 Four-poster bedstead covered with material. Bedsteads with the woodwork entirely covered with material were used as early as the beginning of the 17th century, though only in mansions. They were revived again towards the end of the century, though the all-wood four-poster still remained popular. Late 17th century.

The bedroom

The wooden bedstead of Jacobean times was replaced by the material-covered type in the William and Mary period, though as early as James I's time the fashion of covering over the woodwork entirely with tapestry, plush, and other materials had become popular – at any rate amongst the people of leisure. One of the rooms at Knole House, Sevenoaks, was refurnished specially in honour of a visit by James I, and the bedstead is of the covered type.

Fig. 34 shows a covered bedstead dating from about 1700. Note that the cornice is made up of a number of short pieces of moulding mitred together, some straight and others curved. The material is strained over these. The actual wood used was generally beech and oak, except the exposed feet which were of walnut.

Other pieces used in the bedroom would be the chest of drawers, usually a tallboy, with which we have already dealt, or a wardrobe or press, in appearance somewhat similar to the secretaire in Fig. 19, but the upper carcase had two doors instead of a fall front.

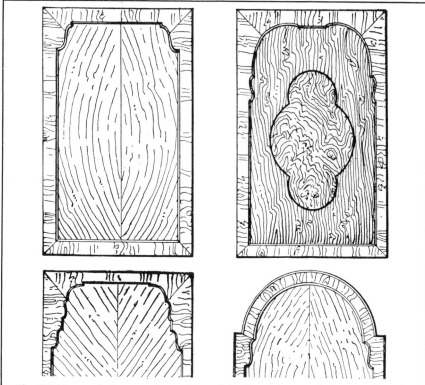

Fig. 35 Veneered doors and panels used in the walnut period. Note that the framework of doors was invariably cross-grained in the veneer. Sometimes the corners were mitred as here, in other cases the veneer of the top and bottom rails was butted between the uprights. Early 18th century.

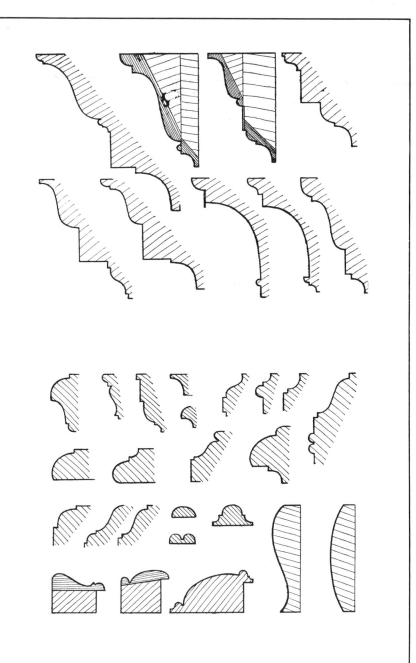

Fig. 36 Moulding sections of the walnut period. Practically without exception the mouldings were cross-grained, a thin slip of walnut being glued to a groundwork of pine or oak. The two centre sections at the top show this. Late 17th and early 18th century.

Fig. 37 Typical walnut period handles.

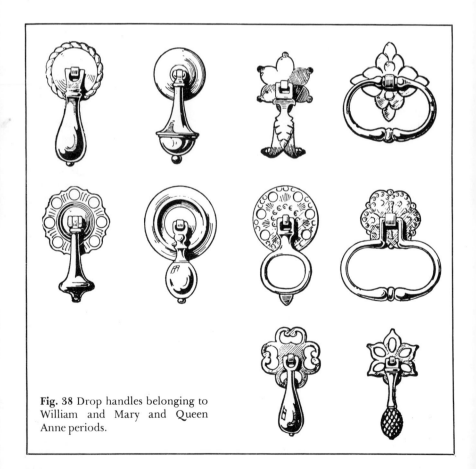

Fig. 38 Drop handles belonging to William and Mary and Queen Anne periods.

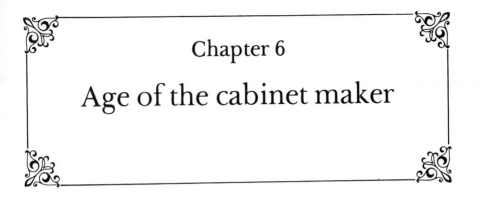

Chapter 6

Age of the cabinet maker

Early Georgian period

This period is remarkable chiefly because mahogany as a furniture wood was first used. As early as 1715 a few pieces were made in mahogany, but it was not in general use until 1725–1730. From 1733 onwards, the tax on imported timber being abolished, mahogany came to be used exclusively. It was imported from the West Indies and was of the kind known as Spanish mahogany, a hard, heavy wood, rather inclined to be brittle, but very reliable. Early specimens were finished with linseed oil, this being coated on liberally and allowed to remain for a few days. A polish was then obtained with brickdust rubbed on with a cork. Later varnish was used.

Although in general proportions and form there was no immediate break from what had been common in the walnut period, there came almost at once many changes in detail and construction. It was not simply that a cabinet maker, used to the walnut tradition, would simply substitute mahogany for walnut, and make it otherwise just the same. There was more in it than that, and the root cause was the fact that, whereas walnut furniture was *always* veneered (except for such parts as legs, which had to be in the solid), mahogany was used in the solid. As a matter of fact such pieces as chairs, which in their nature had to be mostly solid, altered less than any other kinds of furniture because the construction was not affected by the change of wood.

It was pointed out in chapter 5 that walnut furniture relied for its decorative effect largely upon the figuring of the grain and upon such details as cross-banding and quartering, which went naturally with veneering. The use of veneer made flat surfaces desirable, and when carving was used at all it was mostly upon the solid parts such as the legs. Now the mahogany first imported was dark, frequently with not particularly interesting figure, and this plainness must have been very obvious to people who were used to the rich figuring of walnut. Then, again, quartering as a means of decoration was impossible for this essentially belonged to veneering. A quartered panel in solid wood

Fig. 1 Mahogany wardrobe and armchair. When mahogany was first introduced there was a return to the solid form of construction and, the grain of the wood being somewhat plain, it became usual to introduce raised panels to give a decorative effect. Note the doors of the wardrobe. About 1730.

would inevitably twist out of shape and split. Cross-banding again, although not impossible in the solid, was not specially desirable, because it would not stand out well as the grain was not strongly marked.

It therefore became obvious to the cabinet makers that a new form of treatment was necessary for mahogany, and as a consequence there was a return to the panelled type of door in which the different levels of the panel and the moulding of the framework broke up what would otherwise have been a wide, uninteresting expanse. Panels were frequently fielded, that is a wide canted rebate was worked around the edges as in the wardrobe in Fig. 1. Carving, too, was revived as a means of decoration, though of a quite different type from that of its last period of popularity in the late seventeenth century.

Fig. 1 shows a press made entirely of solid mahogany (except for such parts as drawer sides and so on which are of oak), and it exemplifies well many of these points. The doors, for example, have grooved-in, fielded panels. Then, again, the drawers stand forward from the front of the carcase and have a thumb moulding worked round, so making their shape well defined, and at the same time helping to make them dustproof. Incidentally the wardrobe in Fig. 1 probably had five drawers originally. The bottom one was probably cut away in Victorian times to reduce the height. In the best class work the mouldings would probably have been carved – they were never cross-grained as in the walnut work for the same reason that cross-banding was discontinued, the grain was too plain to stand out.

Presses of this kind became general in this first half of the eighteenth century. They were exceptionally deep and gave excellent accommodation. The upper portion was generally fitted with oak trays made to slide forwards, extension runners being fitted to the inside of the doors to give support when withdrawn. Sometimes the doors had what is known as the rule joint at the hingeing edge. It was a similar arrangement to that used in the tops of gate-leg tables of Jacobean times, the sides of the cupboard having a quarter-round shape or moulding at the front edge, and the door a corresponding hollow, so that the one worked in the other as the door was opened. It had its value from the decorative point of view, though the reason for its use was mainly a technical one, since it made the doors flush with the inner surfaces of the sides when opened, so enabling the trays to slide closely between them.

The chair is typical of the upholstered form made at the time. Note that the winged sides and scrolled arms are similar to those of Queen Anne's time (compare it with the walnut chair in Fig. 13, page 93). One feature in which it differs is the carving on the knees and feet of the cabriole legs. This takes the form of a lion's head and paw, details used for the first time in the early Georgian period. Other new *motifs* were the eagle heads with claw feet, masks, and the cabochon detail which resembled the detail of a precious stone cut without facets. At the same time the claw and ball foot continued to be popular, as shown in the dining chair in Fig. 3. Note that here a new detail is the carving of the

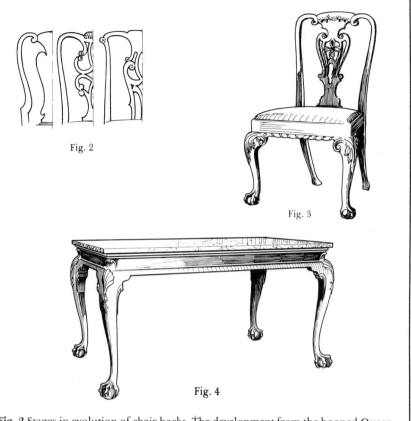

Fig. 2

Fig. 3

Fig. 4

Fig. 2 Stages in evolution of chair backs. The development from the hooped Queen Anne shape with urn splat.

Fig. 3 Mahogany chair with cabriole legs carved with acanthus leaf-work. About 1730.

Fig. 4 Mahogany side table with marble top and cabriole legs. Although made in mahogany this table has many features belonging to the walnut period, particularly in the shells and pendant husks carved on the knees of the cabriole legs. About 1730.

knee, which takes the form of acanthus leaf-work scrolling from the ear pieces down to the centre.

Fig. 2 is of particular interest in that it shows the development from the full Queen Anne rounded back to the straight top rail in common use by the middle of the century. In the left-hand example the upright has the typical inward sweep immediately above the seat, and at the top it has a fairly full round sweeping towards the centre. Note, too, that the splat is solid. In the next example the inward sweep is omitted in the uprights, and the curve at the top has become more acute. The splat, too, is pierced. In the third illustration the top rail is more or less flat and the upright has only the slightest curve.

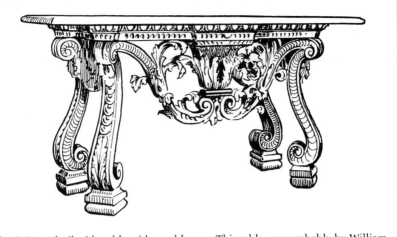

Fig. 5 Carved gilt side table with marble top. This table was probably by William Kent, an architect who designed furniture for his houses. It was of an elaborate kind, architectural in character, and a complete departure from the traditional kind generally made at the period. About 1735.

In these early Georgian days there was no such thing as a sideboard. Instead a side table was used, this usually having a marble top, as in the example in Fig. 4. This, although made in mahogany and dating from about 1730, has typical 'walnut' features, especially in the use of the carved shell and husks on the cabriole legs. We shall see later that the sideboard, as we now know it, was evolved from the side table, separate pedestals first being added to give better accommodation. Later these were joined up to make a single piece. The illustration on page 12 shows the stages of evolution through which it passed.

An architect who began to make a name for himself in George I's reign was William Kent, and as he designed a certain amount of furniture for his houses we may conveniently take note of his work here. Kent had travelled in Italy, and on his return was an enthusiastic follower of the Palladian style which had become fashionable in architecture. He was a man of considerable ability, but so far as his furniture was concerned he seemed to strike a foreign note in the scheme of things. It was of a ponderous, extravagant kind, rather the sort of thing one might expect to find in the entrance hall of a theatre than in an ordinary dwelling house. Elaborately scrolled legs, bold masses of carving, heavy classical mouldings, marble tops, and the free use of gilding all seem to suggest that the work would have been better carried out in marble rather than wood.

Fig. 5 shows a side table in the Kent style in which this magnificent treatment is exemplified. It is the work of an architect not familiar with the technique of woodwork. No practical cabinet maker would ever have attempted to design such a piece, and it in no way represents a stage in the evolution of the sideboard. It is just the work of an individualist and seems to fall outside the general scheme of things.

Fig. 1 Mahogany Chippendale chair. Mahogany chair with a back based on a pattern in Chippendale's *Director*, probably made c. 1760. It is one of a set of chairs in the collection of Lord St. Oswald at Nostell Priory. About 1760.

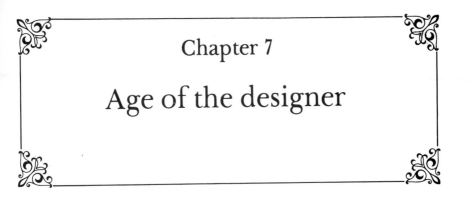

Chapter 7

Age of the designer

Chippendale period

It is as well to realize at the outset that the title of this chapter, the Age of the designer, is one largely of convenience, and must not be accepted without certain qualifications. That it implies an age when certain men were working out styles in an individual way is perfectly true, but it does not mean that these were the only men working in those styles; neither does it mean that they were necessarily the originators of them. This may sound somewhat a paradox, but the case is simple when one comes to analyse it.

Take two outstanding designers, Thomas Chippendale and George Hepplewhite. Both these names have come to stand for certain styles in furniture, and a chair, or whatever it may be, can be picked out and dubbed as one or the other. But this does not necessarily imply that it was made by either of these cabinet makers. When one comes to consider the vast amount of mahogany furniture of the period which has survived (discounting the many fakes and reproductions) it must be obvious that *all* of it could not possibly have been made in the workshops of just two firms. That both firms prospered and turned out a good deal of furniture is true, but against this was the fact that it was all made entirely by hand, so that the labour and time involved must have been tremendous.

It becomes obvious then that, taking just this aspect of the case, there must have been many cabinet makers who were making furniture in these styles, and we have now to consider whether these were plagiarists copying the ideas of just two men, or whether the names Chippendale and Hepplewhite have come to be applied to certain furniture merely because these two fashionable cabinet makers happened to be working in styles which had evolved naturally. Opinion on the subject has changed considerably during the last twenty-five to thirty years. Chippendale used to be held up as a great designer and practical cabinet maker, so great and individual in style that the whole trade automatically turned to him as a leader and copied his works in sheer admiration. Today people are more cautious in accepting this theory.

Both Chippendale and Hepplewhite were practical cabinet makers. Their places of business are known to have been in London, the former in St. Martin's Lane and the latter in Cripplegate, and both published books of designs. Possibly it was these books that gave rise to the theory that they were the leaders of design, the fact being lost sight of that these were virtually catalogues. The more likely theory is that both men were extremely successful interpreters of styles which were a natural development along traditional lines. In the sense that both were able, practical cabinet makers, with a gift of originality, they helped to establish styles on thoroughly sound traditional lines and at the same time impart to their work a feeling of individuality. Apart from this, it can hardly be claimed that either was a great designer, turning out purely original work in the way that, say, Wren designed buildings which were entirely individual and obviously the work of a great inventive genius. In fact the firm of Chippendale made furniture to the design of Adam, and we have the curious paradox that, although it was made by Chippendale it is in fact Adam.

The case of Robert Adam as a designer of furniture is in a rather different category. Adam was an architect, not a practical cabinet maker, and he designed his furniture specially to suit the houses he built. It was natural, then, that his furniture should show more of a definite break from tradition, because he was not fettered by years of training in a certain established school (with whatever advantages and disadvantages that carries with it). At the same time, the fact that he became an extremely successful architect with a large clientele made it inevitable that he should attract the attention of many cabinet makers, who would make furniture which was either a copy of pure Adam work or was just founded upon it. Thus, except for certain authentic specimens, one cannot hope to do more than classify a piece as being in the style of Adam.

The Chippendale period

With this explanation of a title which might otherwise be regarded as misleading we may turn our attention to the first school of design, which began at about the time when the second rising for the house of Stuart took place, 1745. We have seen that by this time mahogany was used exclusively – that is, so far as the towns were concerned. There still was a certain amount of oak furniture made in country districts, but it was mainly in the style of years before and cannot be said to be typical of the period. It has also been noted that in some respects the Queen Anne feeling was retained, especially in the pieces which had always been made in solid wood. In particular, the chair still had much in it that was reminiscent of early times, although the gradual flattening of the top rail and the straightening of the uprights had introduced a new element.

Taken generally, the early Georgian period was disappointing from

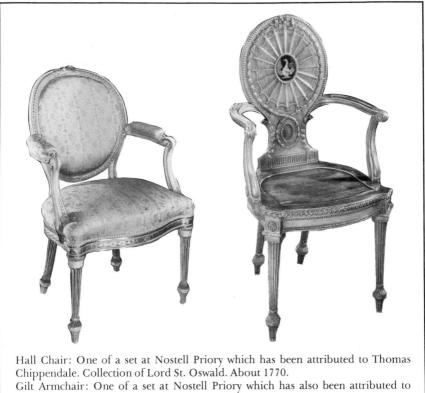

Hall Chair: One of a set at Nostell Priory which has been attributed to Thomas Chippendale. Collection of Lord St. Oswald. About 1770.
Gilt Armchair: One of a set at Nostell Priory which has also been attributed to Thomas Chippendale. Collection of Lord St. Oswald. About 1770.

the point of view of design. It is to be admitted that design is largely a matter of individual taste. One man can find satisfaction in work that has no appeal to another. At the same time the models of about 1730 make a poor showing when compared with the best work of Queen Anne's time, especially in the chairs. Chair making then, as today, had become largely a specialized job, and for some curious reason the craftsmen somehow failed to make the best of their opportunities. Not that the work was generally inferior in the quality of the workmanship; the carving was often of a high order; but that the outlines and general shapes were often poor. For instance, the cabriole leg often degenerated into an overshaped thing, and the claw and ball foot lost a great deal of its former vigour. The shapes of the backs, too, were often unsatisfactory and give one the impression that in feeling round for a new expression the craftsmen were lacking in appreciation of a well-balanced line, good craftsmen though they might be.

By 1745 or so there was a definite upward tendency again. This has often been put down to the advent of Chippendale. That his individual work was generally of a high order, showing a fine appreciation of line backed up by the best craftsmanship, is true, and in that sense he probably did influence the trade, but it is doubtful whether this alone could have been the guiding force in the whole world of cabinet making. It is too much to expect that his influence could have become general in so short a time and extend all over the country. The probable truth is that that particular age produced a number of men all largely gifted with an eye for good proportions and line. It is difficult to explain just why this should have been, but parallel cases happen in all the arts and crafts at certain periods. They lapse for a while and then a whole number of capable men come along, and the art is lifted from the rut into which it seemed to be sinking.

Chippendale's Director   We may, at this point, turn to what little we know of Chippendale himself. This is derived chiefly from his book, *The Gentleman and Cabinet-maker's Director,* first published in 1754, and from bills for goods supplied by him. His workshop was first in Conduit Street, Long Acre, and afterwards in St. Martin's Lane, and it is apparent that he conducted a very flourishing and fashionable business. It appears that in 1755 fire broke out, and a notice of the event states that there were twenty-two workmen's chests in the shop. When one adds to this the men who would have been engaged in polishing, fitting, and general work it is apparent that a great deal of work must have been turned out. Later in his life (he died in 1779) he made a good deal of furniture to the designs of Robert Adam.

That he himself was a practical carver and cabinet maker there is no doubt, and this makes it all the more remarkable that so many of the designs in his book were impractical. It is to be admitted that the plates were the work of an engraver who may have used considerable licence but, even so, it is difficult to conceive a practical man passing designs which he must have known could not have been made as they were. From the preface of a later edition it is apparent that many people of the time had their doubts as to the practicability of some of the designs, for he makes a sort of apology, and attributes the adverse criticisms to 'malice, ignorance, and inability'. Possibly there was something in it. No man becomes successful without somebody feeling the jaundice of jealousy, but all the same Chippendale would have had his work cut out had he had to make some of the items exactly as they appeared in his book.

In some rare instances it has been possible to identify pieces of furniture with illustrations from the *Director* and the differences where the practical cabinet maker has had to adapt the design are obvious. Probably the truth is that the book was intended primarily as a catalogue which would attract men of wealth to the workshop. The list of subscribers includes many titled people and rich merchants, who would be likely to have money to spend, and these were the objective of the book; people who would turn over the leaves and make a selection of things they would order from him.

It is true that the book was also described as a trade book which would include directions for making the various pieces. In the event the main bulk of the subscribers were cabinet makers (this probably accounts for the defensive preface he wrote for his second edition), but from Chippendale's own point of view these were probably incidental to the main object.

Chairs

The middle and second half of the eighteenth century has often been called the golden age of cabinet making, and it was in this Chippendale period that it blossomed. As a first example, take the armchair shown in Fig. 2. It represents a type that has never been excelled. Individual taste may prefer, say, the fine shield back chair of the Hepplewhite school (and certainly that is beautiful enough), but in its own particular way this Chippendale chair has all the parts that go to making a really fine piece, satisfying in line, sound in construction, and of the finest workmanship.

In many ways this chair is a direct descendant from the Queen Anne models with which we are already familiar. Other influences were to creep in later, but here almost every detail has something about it that shows its origin in the traditional line. The legs are of the cabriole type and have the turned club foot used as early as the late seventeenth century. They are finely proportioned, with the full, high knee completely free from the overdone, bandy shape often found in earlier mahogany work. The knee carving is of acanthus leafage, which was the first stage of development from the shell and husk detail of Queen Anne models. The back is the culmination of the stages of evolution shown in Fig. 2, chapter 6. The uprights have only a slight curve – both backwards and sideways – the combined effect of which is to give a sort of serpentine shape when seen from the three-quarter view. The right-hand upright shows this clearly. The top rail is straight (the word is used in contrast with the full rounded shape of Queen Anne models), and the slight dip at the ends gives an acute corner. This detail should be compared with those in Fig 2, page 116. Tradition, too, is preserved in the retention of the single splat in the back, though it is pierced and carved to give the effect of a series of interlacing straps and scrolls. For a fuller analysis of the chair see page 228.

An innovation of the Chippendale period was that of the square leg. In some cases it was completely plain, but as a rule it was moulded along its length as in the chair in Fig. 3. In section the moulding was usually a double ogee, and at the top it was cut away to leave a plain flat surface to which the upholstery materials could be fixed. It should be noted that in this type of chair the stretcher rails are introduced once again. The shaping of the back is similar to that in Fig. 2, though the splat is rather more reminiscent of an earlier pattern like that in Fig. 2, page 116.

At the same time that these fine chairs were being made for the fashionable people in town, a simpler form was being turned out in country districts. Sometimes these were in mahogany, but quite a number were made in beech or even oak and stained to resemble

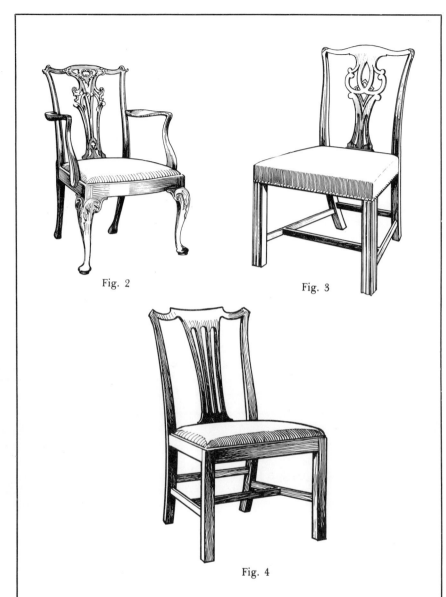

Fig. 2

Fig. 3

Fig. 4

Fig. 2 Armchair with flattened top back rail. The tendency to replace the rounded or hooped back by the flattened top rail is shown in its culmination in this chair. About 1755.

Fig. 3 Chair with square-moulded legs. When this square form of leg was introduced, the stretchers were once again used. The double ogee section of the legs was used almost exclusively. About 1760.

Fig. 4 Simple mahogany chair. For less wealthy customers plain chairs were made which in a general way followed the prevailing fashion but with costly carving and other detail omitted. They were sometimes made in beech. 1760–1770.

Fig. 5

Fig. 6

Fig. 7

Fig. 5 Ladder-back armchair. The back is a departure from the upright slat type which had been used almost exclusively since Queen Anne's time. It was probably a resurrection of the tall ladder-back of Jame II's time. About 1760.

Fig. 6 Mahogany ladder-back dining chair of about 1760. It is the simplest type of chair. Note that shaping of the back occurs in side elevation only, at the front the uprights merely taper towards the top.

Fig. 7 Chair with Chinese influence. This is shown in particular in the use of the lattice work in the back and the frets in the rails. At best it was but a grafting of Oriental detail on to a purely Western form. About 1760.

mahogany. Fig. 4 shows a chair of this kind. The legs are plain and the back splat has the simplest possible piercing. As a rule these chairs have a certain coarseness and heaviness about them, and are obviously the effort of a man working in an unfamiliar element.

A particularly effective pattern of chair was the ladder-back shown in Fig. 5. It was a completely new departure so far as the cabinet maker was concerned, though it may have had its origin in some of the tall back chairs made in the latter part of Charles' II reign. These often had a series of plain horizontal slats, with shaped edges fitting between turned uprights. In the present chair the slats are pierced as well as shaped, and are fitted to the characteristic curved uprights. It will be seen that the same straight moulded legs are used as in Fig. 3, and the curious fact may be noted here that, except for one or two occasional variations, the same pattern of moulding is practically always used in these chairs. It seems rather odd that a trade convention, or whatever it may be called, was so strong that almost every chairmaker followed it. Another simple type of ladder-back chair is that in Fig. 6.

Chinese influence A rather curious influence that took a considerable hold on the world of furniture after the middle of the century was the Chinese. There was a popular rage for things oriental at the time; walls were covered with Chinese wall-papers, and Chinese pottery was in demand. Sir William Chambers had made a visit to China and on his return published a book of drawings of oriental studies. Its effect on furniture was the introduction of such *motifs* as temples, bells, lattice work, and elaborate frets, the whole often being seasoned with a strong French feeling. In mirror frames especially the intermingling of the Chinese and French was strongly marked. A chair having its origin in the popularity of this Chinese style is shown in Fig. 7. Note in particular the detail in the back and the frets of the rails. Furniture treated in this way is often spoken of as Chinese Chippendale, but it will be realized that it is only a rather bizarre adaptation of a few Eastern *motifs* to typical Western work and is not really Chinese in feeling. Chippendale shows a number of chairs of this kind in his book (see also Fig. 16).

The same thing may be said to apply to another passing craze, the Gothic. For some strange reason people began to have a liking for the details belonging to Gothic work of a couple of centuries or so before and Gothic arches, grouped pillars with capitals, trefoils, and so on, suddenly found their way into chairs, tables, and other pieces. Not that people had any liking for the true spirit of Gothic work, the term Gothic was really one of contempt, but it appealed to a passing fancy to pick isolated details here and there and to weave them into the work. At best the result was a mere travesty, and it fell out of favour as quickly as it had come.

Our last example of a chair is that in Fig. 8, which shows a small upholstered armchair of about 1755–60. An interesting feature here are the small fretted corner pieces fitted in the angles of the front legs. These

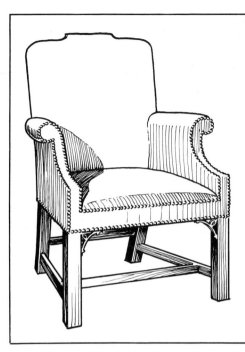

Fig. 8 Upholstered armchair. Note that the back has lost the winged form seen in the last example of an upholstered chair in **Fig. 13**, page 93. Small fretted brackets between the front legs and seat rail were often used as in this example. About 1760.

were often used on the square leg type of chair and on other pieces having similar legs.

Settees   The Queen Anne settee with double or triple back has already been mentioned. Fig. 9 shows its development in the early Chippendale period. There is a great deal about it that is strongly reminiscent of the walnut period, especially in the rounded shaping of the back and the arms with their acutely scrolled front corners. The shell detail, too, is retained in the top rail of the back, and the splats, although pierced, have in their general outline something that can be traced back to the Queen Anne urn shape.

It will probably be felt that there is something unsatisfactory about the back. The centre section is well balanced enough, but those at the sides are uneven because the main side uprights are different from the curves of the wide inner uprights. This difficulty was sometimes overcome, especially in later Chippendale models, by making the inner uprights double, each part being a replica of the main outer upright.

Chippendale tables

We saw in the last chapter that, apart from the William Kent productions, side tables usually had cabriole legs and were often fitted with marble tops. A tendency was to introduce an elaborate apron piece between the front legs, this usually being pierced right through and carved with

Fig. 9 Mahogany settee with back taking the form of three chair backs. There is still something strongly reminiscent of the walnut period in the back, especially in the sweep of the intermediate uprights (not the splats). Altogether the effect is rather unsatisfactory as the two outer sections of the back are not balanced. About 1745.

acanthus leafwork intricately scrolled and intertwined. It rapidly began to grow out of all proportions until the beginning of the Chippendale period.

Fig. 10 shows a small table of simple form and of special interest in that it shows a revival of veneering. In fact it may be mentioned here that a great deal of veneering was done in Chippendale pieces, probably as an economy in the finely-figured woods then being imported. It was, however, usually of a different spirit from that of the Queen Anne period, when the veneer usually hid entirely the construction. In Chippendale work no attempt is made as a rule to hide the construction, and any detail is usually subservient to obtaining good strength.

The difference came about in this way. A Queen Anne cabinet maker would make the framework of, say, a door and would veneer it so that the latter ran right across the joints, concealing them entirely. In Chippendale's time the cabinet maker used far thicker veneer, about 3 mm. ($\frac{1}{8}$ in.), and generally veneered his parts before jointing and putting them together. In this way the joints were bound to show, and it involved no practical difficulty because the veneer was thick enough to allow the joints to be levelled with the plane after being put together, a thing which would have been quite impracticable when the veneer was thinner.

The table in Fig. 10 is rather an exception to this general rule in that the top rail was veneered after it had been jointed to the legs. It is easy to tell this because the veneer runs across both rail and legs. Cross-grained veneer is the exception rather than the rule in Chippendale work, though in a case like this advantage was taken of the fine figuring to show it at its

Fig. 10 (above) Simple side table with moulded legs. The straight leg moulded along its length was used considerably by the Chippendale school. Note that the inner corners are deeply chamfered. About 1760.

Fig. 11 (below) Side table with fret decoration, and small tripod table. The large side table was used in the dining-room to hold dishes and other table furniture, the sideboard as we know it not yet having appeared. A variety of smaller tables such as the tripod type was made for occasional use in the drawing-room. About 1760.

best. The legs are of the straight moulded type already noted, and are deeply chamfered at the inner corners to lighten the appearance.

Use of frets   Another table showing typical Chippendale features is that in Fig. 11. It has the square moulded legs with deep chamfer, and the rails are decorated with frets. This form of ornament was originally derived from the Chinese style. In its purely Chinese form it consisted of intersecting straight lines somewhat in the form of lattice work (see the chair back in Fig. 7), but the idea once prompted soon developed into a purely Western conventional design consisting of curves and scrolls. In Fig. 20, page 137 is given a group of typical Chippendale frets, some still distinctly Chinese in character, and others of the conventional English form.

These frets, when in similar positions to that in the table in Fig. 11, were later applied – that is, they were not carved out of the solid wood, though often enough the ends of scrolls and other small details were touched up with carving tools to give a more realistic appearance of carved work. In some cases the frets had no backing. For instance, little galleried edgings were often fitted to small tables. These were pierced right through in the form of a fret. The cabinet makers soon found that these had little strength when cut out of a single thickness because the grain was necessarily short in certain parts. Consequently they hit upon the idea of gluing together three or more pieces of veneer, the grain of the centre layer running at right angles to those outside. Frets cut in this were considerably stronger. This is probably the first example of the use of plywood, though of course it had little in common with the large plywood panels produced today.

Side tables, such as that in Fig. 11, would be placed in the dining-room, and their purpose was to provide a useful standing space for the dishes. The day of the sideboard with drawer and cupboard accommodation had yet to come. The reader may care to turn to Fig. 12 to see examples of other kinds of legs used in tables of this kind. The second example is interesting in that it is pierced right through, a detail which came from the Chinese influence. One entirely new form of leg is the fourth example which is composite, that is, built up of a number of small separate pieces. It consists of a series of clusters of turned columns fitted between squares. Quite light tables had this form of leg.

Many new kinds of occasional tables made their appearance at this time, and amongst them was the small tripod form also shown in Fig. 11. The simpler examples were quite plain, consisting of three legs (like that at Fig. 12F), joined to a turned centre upright, and a circular top. Finer specimens as that in Fig. 11 had acanthus carving on the knees of the legs and on the turned upright. The edge of the top, too, was often 'piecrusted'. This piecrust edging was always carved in the solid. The recessed centre part was recessed on the lathe leaving just the edging to be fretted out to shape and carved to a moulded section. In cheap reproduction tables the moulded edging is applied, being first spindle moulded then mitred and glued on.

Bureaux and writing tables

We saw in chapter 5 how the great increase in writing led to the introduction of pieces intended specially for writing. Of these the bureau (usually with the bookcase above) and the writing table remained popular. The secretaire in its original form, with huge fall writing top, lapsed, though a certain number of pieces with comparatively small falls were made. These were similar to the bureau except that the fall when closed was upright. When opened out flat the whole writing arrangement could be pulled forward giving easy access to the stationery nest.

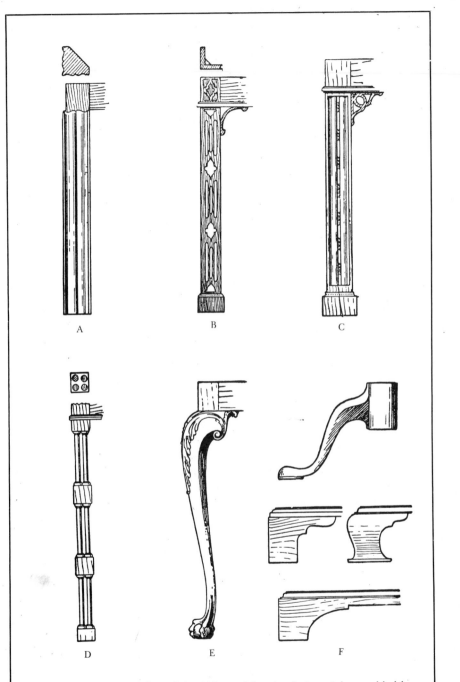

Fig. 12 Typical legs and feet of the Chippendale school. A straight moulded leg; B fretted leg; C straight moulded and carved leg; D grouped pillar leg; E cabriole leg; F tripod leg, and bracket feet. 1750–1775.

Fig. 13 Simple bureau in mahogany. The drawer fronts are edged with a corked bead, and at the front corners quarter-round turned pillars are inset. About 1760.

Fig. 14 Writing desk with leather covered top. The moulding above the knee space is carved, a common feature of Chippendale work. This would have been impossible in walnut work because the moulding was built up with a thin layer of walnut. About 1765.

A simple Chippendale bureau is given in Fig. 13. It is similar in general form to its predecessor of Queen Anne's time, though, apart from being in mahogany, the decorative treatment is entirely different. Sometimes the sides, drawer fronts, and so on were veneered, about 3 mm. ($\frac{1}{8}$ in.) thick, but there was no ruling on the subject. In any case, when veneer was used the front was simply regarded as a solid piece with a facing of mahogany; that is to say, there was no attempt to use the veneer to give a

Fig. 15 Detail of a mahogany library table supplied by Thomas Chippendale. In the collection of Lord St. Oswald at Nostell Prior. 1767.

decorative effect as in walnut work. No quartering or cross-banding was used. Drawers were usually surrounded by a cocked bead, as in the present example. For interior parts, drawer sides, etc., oak was generally used.

Another bureau similar in form, but with bookcase above, is shown in Fig. 17. The bookcase has many typical features, of which the pediment with carved rosettes and fretted underpart, and the barred doors are the most obvious. These barred doors were a continuation of the Queen Anne type (see Fig. 21, page 100), which probably owed their origin to the comparatively small sizes in which glass was first available. All the panes are separate and fit between bars consisting of a moulding, usually an astragal, with a thin flat bar at the back to form rebates for the glass. A few other Chippendale patterns of barred doors are given in Fig. 19. Both these bureaux are of simple form. Note the use of bracket feet in both. These were used almost universally in these pieces, though in finer specimens they were often finely carved. More elaborate specimens had pilasters flanking the doors with fine carving in them and had altogether more elaborate pediments.

A writing table is shown in Fig. 14. In this we have a variation of the bracket foot, the solid plinth. Note that certain of the mouldings are carved. This was a revival which took place in the mahogany period. In the earlier oak days carving was used to decorate mouldings to a

Fig. 16 Chinese Chippendale writing table in mahogany. Note how the front legs are divided, the front portions pulling forward and supporting the box-like drawer on which the writing top slides. Collection of Lord St. Oswald at Nostell Priory. About 1760.

Fig. 17 Bureau bookcase and writing table. Typical features in the left-hand example are the barred doors and shaped pediment with fretted detail beneath. The writing table is of a kind that became popular early in the century. 1760–1770.

Fig. 18 Writing table in mahogany about 1760. The front legs are divided diagonally in section, the front portion pulling forward with the rail and increasing the writing surface.

considerable extent, but it lapsed entirely in walnut furniture because in this the mouldings were invariably cross-grained. This produced a decorative effect in itself, but it was not practical to carve them because the cross-grain was simply a thin layer glued over a solid groundwork. With the return to the use of solid wood in the first half of the eighteenth century carving was once again possible, though it was on altogether finer lines than that of oak work. A smaller writing table with knee hole space is given in Fig. 17. Fig. 15 shows one end of a library table, and reveals the magnificent detail of what is a first quality piece of furniture, actually made in the Chippendale workshop. Note that the surround to the elliptical panel is quartered, this of course being in veneer. An altogether lighter table, Fig. 16, is a good example of Chinese style.

A type of table often known as an architect's table is that in Fig. 18, but its purpose was probably that of writing. The steward of a country mansion would probably use it for such things as accounts.

Fig. 19 Barred doors of Chippendale school. Nearly all bookcases had barred doors. The moulding was usually a small astragal with stiffening bar at the back forming rebates for the glass. 1750–1775.

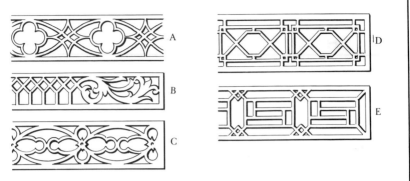

Fig. 20 Chippendale frets. **A, B** and **C** are conventional patterns of Western form. **D** and **E** show the Chinese influence. 1760–1775.

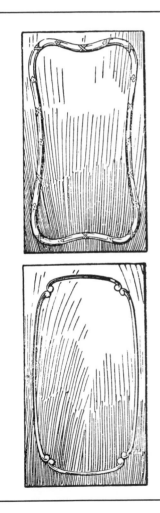

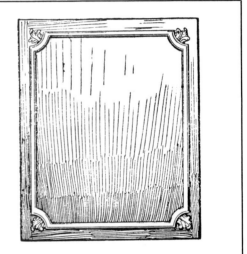

Fig. 21 Door and panels used in Chippendale work. Generally the door was made of a framework with separate panel as in top right example. In other cases the panel was framed in flush and the whole thing veneered, the moulding, either shaped and carved or in the form of scrolls, being planted on the face. 1750–1775.

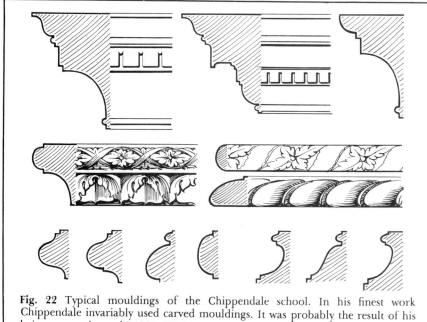

Fig. 22 Typical mouldings of the Chippendale school. In his finest work Chippendale invariably used carved mouldings. It was probably the result of his being a carver by trade. 1750–1775.

Fig. 23 Simple mahogany chest of drawers. Although of plain form this simple furniture was, as a rule, thoroughly well made. It was the sort of thing that the merchant class would have used. 1760–1770.

Bedroom furniture

The chest of drawers, established by Queen Anne's time, was a recognized part of the furnishing of a Georgian bedroom. In its simplest form it was often severely plain with no decoration. The drawers usually had a surrounding cocked bead, but even these were primarily utilitarian, since their chief purpose was to protect the edges of the veneer. An example of this simple furniture is given in Fig. 23. The chamfered front corners are worth noting because, although in this particular example they are quite plain, in better class pieces they were often developed as an important feature, carving, fluting, or frets often being used as decoration. A chest of this kind would have been used in the house of one of the middle classes or in one of the lesser bedrooms in an important house.

In contrast is the fine chest of drawers or commode shown in Fig. 24. A piece of this kind represents the high water mark in cabinet work, and is obviously the product of a first-class workshop. It is distinctly French in character, and is probably taken from a Louis XV commode except that, whereas the latter would be largely gilded (probably the mountings of the legs would be of metal), in the present example they are entirely in mahogany, showing its natural surface. A feature adding considerably to the difficulty of making such a piece is the fact that it has compound

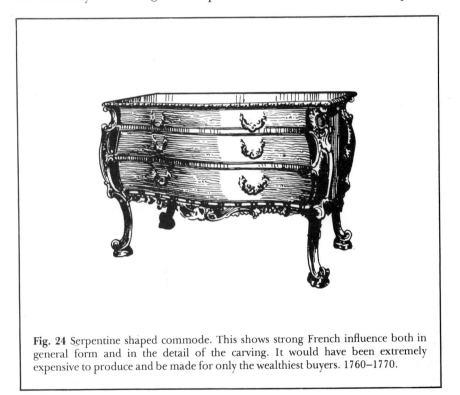

Fig. 24 Serpentine shaped commode. This shows strong French influence both in general form and in the detail of the carving. It would have been extremely expensive to produce and be made for only the wealthiest buyers. 1760–1770.

Fig. 25 Four-poster bedstead in the style of Chippendale. After the walnut period the bedstead covered entirely with material fell into disfavour, and the woodwork was again exposed. About 1760.

shaping; that is, in addition to being of serpentine shape in plan, it is shaped in its height. This double shaping was often used in Louis XV work for the French were a long way ahead of us in work of this type – possibly because very elaborate work has never specially appealed to us. Other features in the chest definitely of French origin are the scrolled legs, with their Rococo ornament and the handles. An enlarged detailed drawing of one of these French type of handles is given in Fig. 28.

Bedsteads The Queen Anne bedstead was for the most part the four-poster type, entirely covered with soft materials, as in the example given in Fig. 34, page 109. A few were made with head and foot and no upper tester, these having a typical Queen Anne shaping at the top of the panel and cabriole legs below. A great many modern reproductions of the type are made today. The majority, however, were four-posters, with every part of the woodwork (except possibly the feet) covered entirely up with velvet and other materials. It was scarcely a thing fit for everyday use in an average house, though it might be well enough in a palace. It was not like a four-poster with curtains only that could be taken down and washed. Once the material became faded or worn nothing short of stripping off the whole would be of the slightest use.

Fig. 26 Chippendale grandfather clock. The domed shape of the hood with a pediment above was invariably used. 1760–1770.

Fig. 27 Pole screen. The screen portion was made so that it could be adjusted at varying heights. About 1765.

Fig. 26

Fig. 27

In Georgian times came a return to the all-wood bedsteads. In a sense these were similar to the four-posters of Jacobean times, but were altogether lighter and were in mahogany instead of oak. A Chippendale example is given in Fig. 25. In some cases the Chinese character was used entirely. There stands in the museum at South Kensington a bedstead of this kind, in which the tester follows the form of a pagoda roof, whilst the back is decorated with lattice work. The whole thing is in gold and black lacquer and was probably made in Chippendale's own workshop.

The development of the grandfather clock is shown in Fig. 26. Note the scrolled pediment above the rounded heading of the hood door.

Simple handle

French influence

Handle with keyhole plate

Early Chippendale

Handle with pierced back plate

Chinese influence

Fig. 28 Various handles and escutcheons of Chippendale furniture.

Carved mirror frame with gilt gesso. The frame would first be carved and covered with a thick layer of gesso. Any fine detail would then be carved in the gesso, and finally the whole water-gilt. About 1760.

Fig. 1 Shield-back chair, about 1775. Illustrations of almost identical chairs appear in Hepplewhite's *The Cabinet Maker and Upholsterer's Guide*. Photograph by courtesy of the Victoria and Albert Museum, London.

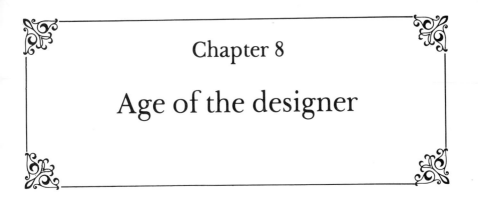

Chapter 8

Age of the designer

Hepplewhite period

Hepplewhite began his career as a cabinet maker at a time when the art of cabinet making was at its fullest tide. The second half of the eighteenth century is often called the golden age of cabinet making, and by 1760, when Hepplewhite settled in business at Cripplegate, the standard of design and craftsmanship was at its zenith. The Chippendale school was still in its prime, and there was a strong group of craftsmen who had ingrained in them a fine trade tradition, a thing which implies something more than a mere ability to use tools. It means a sense of appreciation and a certain element of originality, tempered with the convention that belongs to a workshop where every thing is done by hand.

George Hepplewhite was one of these practical men. He was scarcely a designer in the sense that Robert Adam was. He did not sit down at his drawing board and sketch out purely original designs, but his work had characteristic features that can usually be recognized. As a cabinet maker he knew his job perfectly and, in addition, he had a keen appreciation of fine line which enabled him to give his work a certain individuality in a way that would be beyond a man of no imagination. In this sense he no doubt influenced the trade considerably, but beyond this he simply worked in a certain style which a group of cabinet makers was following. His name has come to be attached to that style probably because of his book, *The Cabinet Maker and Upholsterer's Guide,* and that was not published until 1788, two years after his death.

It is apparent, then, in speaking of Hepplewhite furniture a general style popular from about 1760 until practically the end of the century is implied rather than the work of Hepplewhite himself as an individual. A great deal of furniture no doubt was made in the workshop at Cripplegate, but except in a few rare instances it is impossible definitely to identify it.

Taken generally, Hepplewhite furniture was comparatively simple. There were a few touches of refined, delicate decoration, but even the most ornate specimens had nothing like the elaboration found in the richer Chippendale pieces. Several new forms of decoration were

145

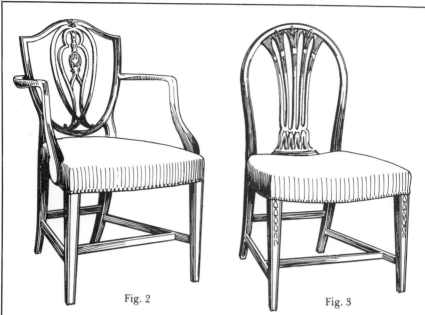

Fig. 2   Fig. 3

Fig. 2 Shield-back chair. One of the finest chairs produced in the 18th century. For all their lightness these chairs were extremely strong, being made in the finest mahogany and of the best workmanship. 1770–1780.

Fig. 3 Hoop-back chair. A favourite motif of Hepplewhite were the ears of wheat. These appear at the top of the pierced splat in the back. 1770–1780.

Fig. 4 Oval-back chair. The French influence is strongly marked in this chair. Except for this French form the cabriole leg was never used by the late 18th century designers. 1770–1780.

introduced or revived, for whereas Chippendale work had little other form of decoration besides carving, Hepplewhite furniture had inlay, painting, and gilding in addition to carving. The inlay usually took the form of bandings and strings in satinwood, rosewood, ebony, and so on, and was in fact very similar to the inlaid work usually associated with Sheraton. Carving was of small classical subjects, vases, festoons, draped cloth, and swags of husks, an entire departure from the elaborate scrolling acanthus leafwork of the Chippendale school.

It is perhaps in the chair that the Hepplewhite characteristic is most marked. Probably the most famous type is the shield-back, of which examples are given in Fig. 1 and 2. A really fine example of a shield-back ranks amongst the most beautiful things ever produced but, like the cabriole leg, first-rate examples are rare. The truth is that it takes a first-class chair maker of considerable experience to make one properly, the difficulty being that the shaping runs in three directions. There is the shield shape seen from the front, the backward rake, and the concave plan shape. To incorporate all these to form one harmonious whole is something that calls for a great deal of skill and experience.

As a rule the main back framing had a channelled moulding worked all round it, and the probable reason for this was that it helped to emphasize the shield shape. It will be realized that, although the lower part of the shield appears to be in one piece, it is in reality in three. The side portions in fact continue down, forming the back legs, and a curved bottom rail is fitted in to complete the shape between them. By channelling the wood the shield appears to be in one unbroken piece. The front legs of these chairs were invariably tapered.

The chief outside influences of Hepplewhite were the Adam and the French. Of the latter there was Louis XV, which showed itself in the cabriole leg exemplified in Fig. 4. Note the French scrolled foot and the flat shaping which continues along the front seat rail in an unbroken sweep. Another French influence came from the Louis XVI, and one result was the use of the turned leg. An example is the settee, Fig. 6.

Other typical Hepplewhite chair backs are the hoop-back, of which Fig. 3 is an example, the oval back, Fig. 4, heart shape, and that with the serpentine shaped top rail curving into the uprights.

Pieces such as sideboards, writing tables, bureaux, chests of drawers, tallboys, wardrobes, and so on were, as already mentioned, extremely like Sheraton furniture, and are dealt with more fully in chapter 10. The bedstead in Fig. 6 is a four-poster, very like one appearing in Hepplewhite's book, and shows the general restraint in treatment.

Fig. 5 is a sideboard belonging to the last few years of the eighteenth century. It has characteristics of the Hepplewhite style, but there are others which belong equally to Sheraton and, as we are dealing with what might be termed schools of design rather than the work of individuals, it is apparent that one can do little more than term it late eighteenth century. It is probably the work of a cabinet maker whose name has not come down to posterity, and worked in the period's traditional style.

Fig. 5 Sideboard with break-front decorated with inlay. It was not until towards the end of the 18th century that the sideboard with drawer and cupboard accommodation was made. It was evolved from the side table with separate pedestals. It is difficult to distinguish between Hepplewhite and Sheraton pieces as both had a great deal in common. Late 18th century.

Fig. 6 Bedstead and settee in Hepplewhite style. The bedstead is very like one appearing in Hepplewhite's book, *The Cabinet Maker and Upholsterer's Guide,* which was published in 1788, after his death. 1770–1780.

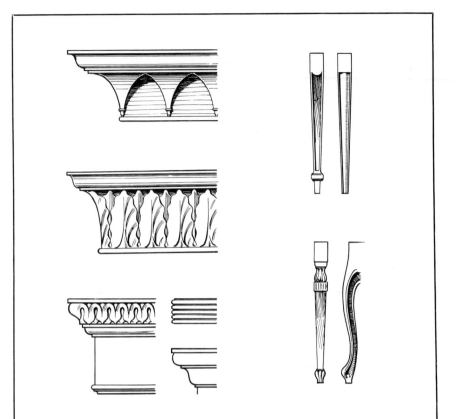

Fig. 7 Hepplewhite mouldings and legs. Mouldings were of a refined character, sometimes finely carved. Legs were mostly square tapered or turned, though the French form of cabriole leg was sometimes used. 1760–1790.

Fig. 1 Door casing at Osterley Park, the work of Robert Adam. Note also the gilt armchair, a typical Adam piece.

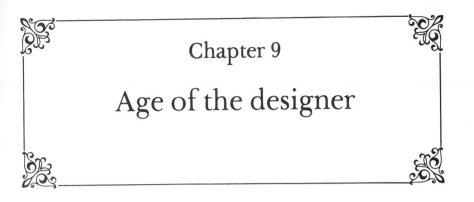

Chapter 9

Age of the designer

Adam period

In one important sense Robert Adam was entirely different from the other outstanding characters with whose work this book deals. He was an architect by profession, not a practical cabinet maker, and in turning his attention to furniture he was not in any way fettered by any convention which a tradesman might have. It is not suggested that the convention of a good trade tradition is bad; it is one of the healthiest influences a craft can have; but it simply is a statement of fact that Adam was able to approach the subject from a fresh angle. He worked from his drawing board and passed on his designs to be carried out by a practical cabinet maker.

He travelled a good deal in France and Italy, and on his return in 1758 he set himself up as an architect and rapidly became very successful. As a result of his foreign studies he was influenced considerably by the classical school, but he had a strong individual turn, and as a result his work had a characteristic touch which made it different from that of other architects working in the classical style. It was delicate and refined, some term it effeminate, abounding in small intricate detail, and it superseded largely the rather heavier work of such architects as Sir William Chambers.

His connection with furniture was that in designing an interior he included the furniture as an essential part of the scheme. To the average architect the work was finished when the walls and ceiling had been decorated, but Adam required every detail, even to the ornaments on the sideboard, to harmonize with his ideas. Perhaps the most notable example is that of Harewood House, in which the furniture was designed by Adam and executed by Chippendale.

Although there were marked characteristics in Adam furniture, one has to be wary in accepting a piece as genuine Adam. The fact that he had to employ practical cabinet makers, combined with his great success, soon led to a great deal of imitation. In fact, of all the 'Adam' work that has survived only a very small part can be identified as owing its origin to

151

Fig. 2 Adam sideboard consisting of separate table and pedestals. The pedestals were introduced to augment the limited accommodation of the table. About 1780.

Fig. 3 Adam sideboard in mahogany with turned and carved vases. Photograph by courtesy of M. Harris & Son.

Adam himself. It is one of the penalties of success (if a complimentary one) that other people quickly begin to copy what a man does and so, although Adam himself was an individual and original designer, Adam furniture was, for the most part, the work of a school working in his style.

Adam used many methods of decoration in his furniture. The carving had definite characteristics. The acanthus leafage was finer and more delicately treated than in the full scrolled form which Chippendale had favoured, and, in addition, he used chains of husks, the honeysuckle device, Greek key, vases, drapery, plaques carved with mythological subjects, rams' heads, and grotesques. Inlay and marquetry, too, were revived, and were carried out in satinwood, tulipwood, rosewood, amboyna, harewood, and so on. The subjects were similar to those of the carving. Another form of decoration was painting in the style of Angelica Kauffman. A popular treatment was to make these painted panels the main feature of a design of scrolling acanthus leafwork and husks. In some few instances, too, Wedgwood plaques were introduced.

A typical Adam sideboard is shown in Fig. 2. Properly speaking, it is a side table with two pedestals, but the three pieces were intended to stand together and form a whole. In some cases the pedestals were actually joined to the table, as in Fig. 3. There was a general tendency to make the sideboard a single unit, in fact, the Sheraton sideboard in Fig. 7, page 162, exemplifies the point.

Fig. 4 Dining-table with flap and pivoted back leg. This is one of a pair of tables intended to be placed together when used for dining. The front rail is in reality a drawer front. It now stands in the Victoria & Albert Museum, South Kensington. About 1775.

Fig. 5 Semi-circular Adam side table. An extremely fine piece of cabinet work carried out in mahogany. The curved top rail is veneered, the grain running crosswise. The centre panel and the oval paterae are typical features. 1770–1780.

The pedestals owed their origin to the lack of accommodation in the side table. If one refers back to the side table of Chippendale's time in Fig. 10, page 129 it is obvious that its only use was to provide standing space on its top. There were no drawers or cupboards in which table funiture could be kept. It fell to Adam to introduce the pedestals. Sometimes they were fitted up with metal grids to enable hot irons to be placed in the cupboards, so providing a means of warming plates. The urns at the top either had metal containers in which iced water was kept, or they were fitted up to hold cutlery. The more ornate specimens were often carved with rams' heads, drapery, husks, and other devices.

Towards the end of the century the cabriole leg practically died right out. In most cases Adam preferred the square tapered leg with small square feet or the turned leg. They were usually recessed in their tapered portion, a pendant of husks often being carved in the recess near the top. The leg at Fig. 6C, shows this detail. Another common treatment was to carve a series of flutes along the length, the lower part often being filled in with reeds (see Fig. 6A).

A particularly fine example of an Adam dining-table is given in Fig. 4. It is one of a pair. In use the two would be placed together, flap to flap, so forming one large table. The flap is supported by a single leg made to

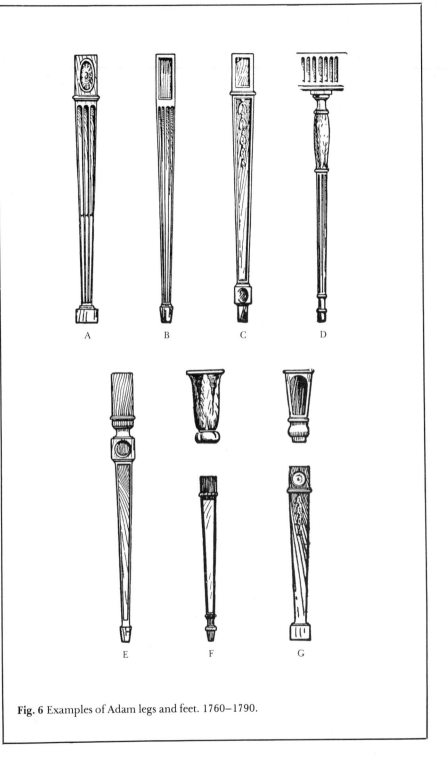

Fig. 6 Examples of Adam legs and feet. 1760–1790.

Fig. 7 Examples of Adam panels and friezes.

Example of an Adam interior. Robert Adam was an architect who became firmly established by about 1760 after extensive travels abroad. He designed a great deal of furniture for his houses, and his style became so popular that many cabinet makers began to imitate it in their own furniture. It follows, then, that only a small number of the pieces which have survived were actually designed by Adam.

pivot. Thus when not required for dining the tables could be placed flat against the wall and become useful side tables. The decorative treatment is well worth noting. The tapered legs are fluted on all sides except one, this being carved with a criss-cross design set in a recess. At the top are paterae carved with leafwork. The fluted top rail with the plain centre part carved with swags of husks is typically Adam. He invariably introduced this centre panel (see also the door casing, Fig. 1).

An example of a small side table with turned and carved legs is given in Fig. 5. It exemplifies well the delicate treatment of which Adam was so fond. Note the use of the centre panel again, this time of quite plain form. Other kinds of Adam legs and feet are given in Fig. 6.

Fig. 1 Painted beechwood armchair. About 1795. Photograph by courtesy of the Victoria and Albert Museum, London.

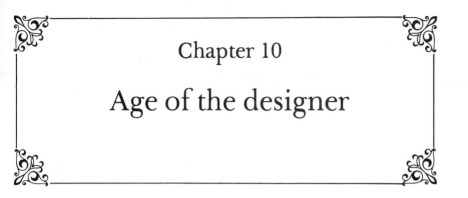

Chapter 10

Age of the designer

Sheraton period

The last of the eighteenth century designers, Thomas Sheraton, came to London from his native town of Stockton-on-Tees about 1790. Although he had undoubtedly been a practical cabinet maker, there is no evidence that he ever made any furniture in London. Certainly he never had a prosperous business such as Chippendale and Hepplewhite had had. His fame in the furniture world rests upon his book, *The Cabinet Maker and Upholsterer's Drawing Book,* published in 1791–94, and appearing in further editions in later years.

It was essentially different from Chippendale's book, the purpose of which was mainly that of a catalogue to appeal to wealthy patrons. Sheraton's drawing book was primarily a trade book intended to help the practical man, not only providing designs but also in supplying a treatise in geometry, perspective and drawing. In the long run it brought him posthumous fame, but as a commercial proposition it was a failure. Probably few practical men were interested in learning to draw in perspective or to know of the problems in geometry (except in the limited way it affected the setting out of their work), and in looking back the whole thing certainly seems an ambitious undertaking.

So far as the designs were concerned, Sheraton certainly showed originality in many of the mechanical movements he introduced and in the design of his chairs, but it must be confessed that the general run of furniture was little more than a representation of the general style prevailing at the time. It was noted in chapter 8 that Hepplewhite and Sheraton furniture, excepting chairs, had a great deal in common; so much so that it is often impossible to say to which it belongs. It will be realized then that in speaking of Sheraton furniture it represents for the most part the work of a school of craftsmen working in a certain style.

In his chairs, however, he undoubtedly did strike an original note. They are lighter than the majority of other late eighteenth century examples, the backs are lower, and instead of the top rail forming a more or less continuous sweep with the uprights (see Fig. 3, page 146) it was

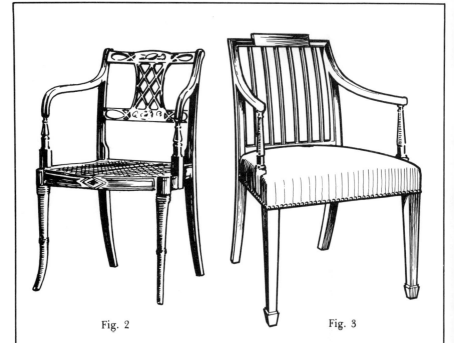

Fig. 2   Fig. 3

Fig. 2 Beechwood armchair painted in black and gilt. The rails of the back have small decorative panels painted with floral and musical instrument subjects. About 1800.

Fig. 3 Mahogany armchair. The backs of Sheraton chairs were usually lower than those of other contemporary work. The sweep of the arms into the back is a characteristic Sheraton touch. Late 18th century.

Fig. 4 Mahogany chair. Sheraton used both square tapered and turned legs. The cabriole type was never used. Late 18th century.

frankly a separate item tenoned between the uprights. The legs were either turned or square tapered (see Fig. 17), and the arms, instead of bowing out sideways, were usually shaped in side elevation only, generally springing from the back in a continuous sweep.

A good example is given in Fig. 2. Note the obvious way in which the back rails fit between the uprights (compare with Fig. 3, page 146), and the sweep of the arms into the uprights. The whole thing is different from anything else being made at the period. The curve of the arms into the turned uprights, the curved legs, and the graceful design of the pierced back are typically Sheraton. It is painted all over (something else that few other designers attempted), and some extremely fine art work is put into the small panels of the back.

Another Sheraton chair, this time with tapered legs, is given in Fig. 3. In this case the arms meet the turned uprights more or less at right angles, but they sweep into the back as in the previous example. The back is practically square, and the uprights which continue down to form the legs are shaped only in side elevation. They are straight when looked at from the front. This is another feature invariably found in Sheraton chairs, and seldom in contemporary work of other designers. All these features also appear in the chair in Fig. 3.

Sheraton died in 1806 and it is unfortunate that towards the end his

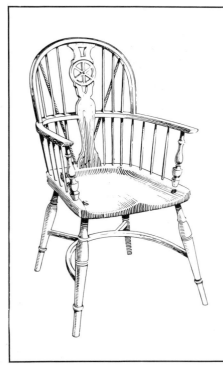

Fig. 6 Wheel back chair. The finest chairs of this kind came from Norfolk and Suffolk. They became popular towards the end of the 18th century, and into the 19th century. Earlier models had curved arm supports at the front instead of turnings. About 1800.

Fig. 7 Sideboard decorated with satinwood inlay bandings. The bow-front sideboard became extremely popular at this time. Sometimes the space between the centre legs was filled in with a cupboard having a tambour front made to slide sideways. Late 18th century.

designs suffered severely. Probably no man, no matter how individual, is quite free from extraneous circumstances. Prevailing fashions exert their sway, and designers are often faced with the choice of either following them or retiring from the scene. Many things were happening in Europe at the close of the eighteenth and beginning of the nineteenth century which were to affect design. The French Revolution, culminating in the establishment of the First Empire, produced a style in France which rapidly found its counterpart this side of the Channel, and the naval victories of this country had an extraordinary effect on furniture. Just as topical events of thirty or forty years ago were commemorated in fretwork designs, so the furniture of the early nineteenth century showed its reaction to the events then happening.

Sheraton fell into the general line and published his *Encyclopaedia* of 1804–07, in which was one of the most extraordinary collections of furniture designs ever put together. Naval emblems of all kinds – anchors, lifebelts, pulley blocks, ropes, and so on, abound, and it is a mercy that more of them were not made up.

To revert to his earlier and happier period, Sheraton's chief form of decoration was inlay. Cross-bandings of fine foreign woods such as satinwood, rosewood, tulip wood, ebony, amboyna, and so on, were inlaid around the edges of drawer fronts and panels, and various built-up patterns in veneer were made use of with great effect. The bow-front sideboard in Fig. 7 shows the use of this cross-banding. Another

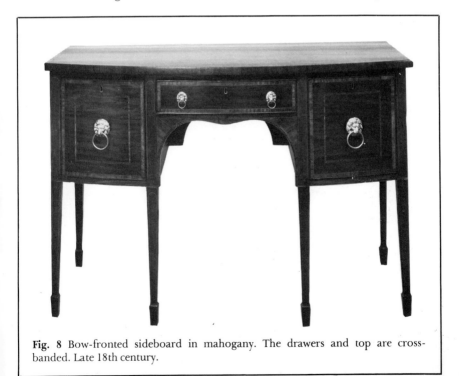

Fig. 8 Bow-fronted sideboard in mahogany. The drawers and top are cross-banded. Late 18th century.

Fig. 9 Mahogany side table with banded drawers. A prominent feature of the Sheraton school was the very limited use of carving. Probably it was a reaction from its free use in the Chippendale period. Late 18th century.

Fig. 10 Circular dining table in mahogany with satinwood cross-banding. The four shaped legs or claws are reeded on the upper surface.

Fig. 11 Two writing desks in mahogany with satinwood bandings. The importation of various foreign fancy woods, satinwood, amboyna, rosewood, ebony and so on led to the free use of these for use in inlay bandings. Satinwood, too, was freely used in the solid, entire pieces being made up in it. Late 18th century.

Fig. 12 Cylinder top writing table and bookcase. The whole is in satinwood enriched with inlay. The cornice is a separate item. End of 18th century.

Fig. 13 Chest of drawers and tallboy decorated with inlay bandings. Late 18th century.

sideboard similar in style and of similar date is that in Fig. 8. Painting he also used considerably, naturalesque floral subjects and panels in the style of Angelica Kauffman being the chief forms it took. Carving he used sparingly and never in the full scrolling form favoured by Chippendale.

A small Sheraton side table is given in Fig. 9. Here again the drawers have an inlaid cross-banding around the edges. The turned legs are reeded down their length. A circular dining-table of late eighteenth century date is that in Fig. 10. Two other Sheraton pieces are given in Fig. 11. Note the inlay again. Desks of this kind were often fitted with elaborate secret contrivances in which stationery boxes, drawers and cupbaords rose up at the touch of a spring. Fig. 12 shows a writing table with bookcase above. It is veneered with satinwood throughout.

Fig. 14 shows a fine inlaid wardrobe in which built-up patterns in veneer are used effectively. The dentils in the cornice and the flutes in the frieze are carried out entirely in inlay. The curved bracket feet are a typical feature of the late eighteenth century. The chair in Fig. 6 is not Sheraton in style, but is a type made by woodturners round about the turn of the century and later, and is so included here.

Fig. 14 Mahogany wardrobe with built-up veneered doors. The fine mahogany imported at this time led to the revival of the built-up patterns in veneer as the grain had splendid decorative value. Late 18th century.

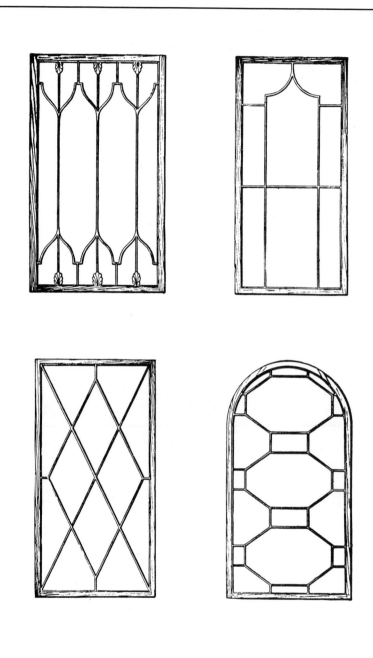

Fig. 15 Sheraton pattern barred doors. Barred doors were used throughout the 18th century. Some of the patterns, notably the twelve-pane shown to the left, bottom row, were used by all the designers of the second half of the century. Late 18th century.

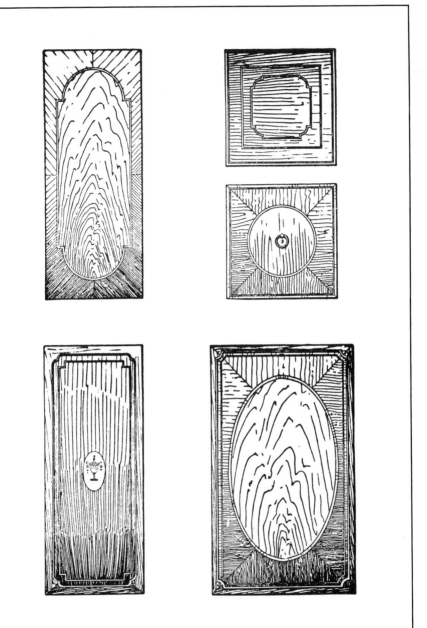

Fig. 16 Examples of doors and panels of the Sheraton period. Built-up designs in veneer were used considerably, and the edges were frequently ornamented with bandings of satinwood, rosewood, ebony and other fancy woods. Late 18th century.

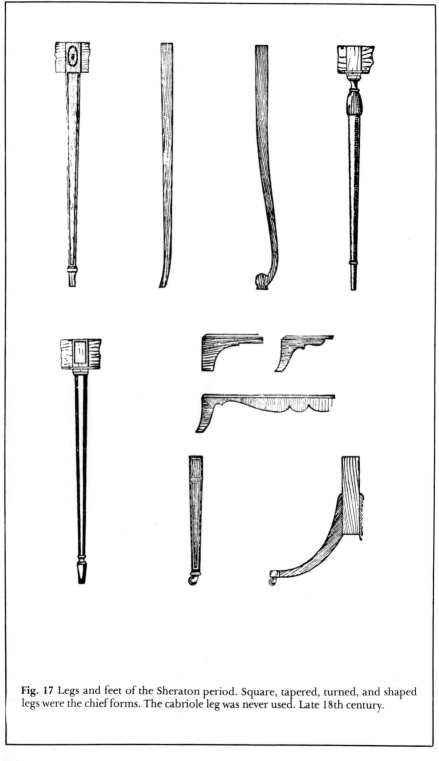

Fig. 17 Legs and feet of the Sheraton period. Square, tapered, turned, and shaped legs were the chief forms. The cabriole leg was never used. Late 18th century.

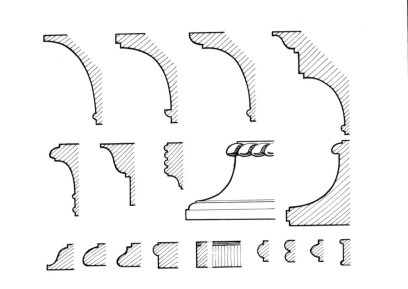

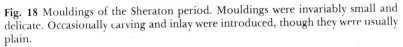

Fig. 18 Mouldings of the Sheraton period. Mouldings were invariably small and delicate. Occasionally carving and inlay were introduced, though they were usually plain.

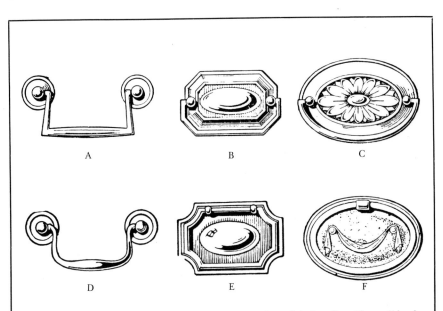

Fig. 19 Examples of handles of the Sheraton period. **A** plain handle with small back plates; **B** favourite octagonal Sheraton form; **C** oval form with patera; **D** shaped handle with small back plates; **E** octagonal type with curved corners; **F** popular oval form.

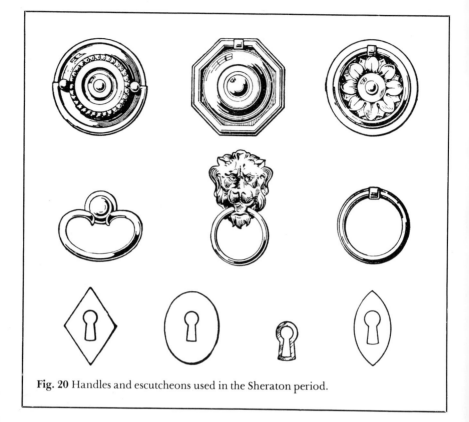

Fig. 20 Handles and escutcheons used in the Sheraton period.

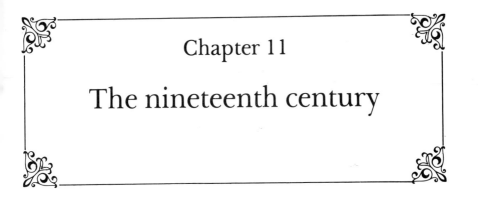

Chapter 11

The nineteenth century

The year 1800 is a convenient date in the history of furniture only in the sense that it marked the beginning of a new century. Apart from that it showed no sudden change in style any more than the start of any other century. The same king was on the throne and was to live for another twenty years, although for the last ten the Prince of Wales was to act as regent. Furthermore, Sheraton, who published his first furniture book in the last decade of the eighteenth century (see page 159), brought out his *Cabinet Dictionary* in 1803, and lived until 1806. Change was taking place, but no more quickly than at any previous period.

At the same time, the period 1800–80 is momentous in that it saw the beginning of the industrial age in which the machine began to replace hand labour. At first its effect was scarcely felt, for the machines themselves were crude and unreliable and had not stood the test of time. Furthermore, no one had had sufficient experience in their use to use them to the best advantage. In any case, their early use was largely confined to Government departments such as shipyards. Being individually built, they were necessarily expensive.

The use of machines speeds up work and reduces costs and that was largely the reason for their introduction. There was, however, another and, in the long run, a deeper-reaching effect. This was the influence on design itself. When you install a machine its first use is invariably to quicken and ease the more back-breaking jobs, such as converting logs, ripping out parts, rough planing them, and so on. Very soon, however, other possibilities are realized, and you see that it can be used for other work which would be difficult or at least expensive by hand. Then comes the idea of adapting the machine for other operations, so that more and more hand work is avoided. At last hand work becomes a thing to be avoided, and then is born that insidious idea of making the design to suit the machine. In a broad sense this is inevitable because any change in technique of manufacture is bound to have its repercussions on design, but the evil comes when sound construction and form are sacrificed to suit the limitations of a machine.

However, up to 1880 there had not been any serious sacrifice in this sense, and during the years about which we are speaking there was a great deal of sound and delightful furniture made, especially in the first twenty years of the century.

For those interested in the subject the following few notes on early machines may be of value. It should be realized, however, that machines were not of necessity power driven. Many of them required human labour to turn them. Even in 1914 some circular saws and bandsaws were still being made which were fitted with handles, and sometimes pedals, which either the operator or an assistant had to work. Sometimes larger saws were propelled by horse labour, the animal being yoked to a bar which revolved a centre pillar, which in its turn was geared to the saw. Water and wind power too were used.

As early as the fifteenth and sixteenth centuries machine saws had been devised, these generally being reciprocating saws worked by cranks. They were exceptional, however, most cutting being done by pairs of sawyers over a saw pit. No doubt the reason for the development of woodworking machines in the nineteenth century was largely due to the tremendous importance of wood as a basic material for all purposes. It was needed for ships, vehicles, houses, some bridges, engineering, agricultural appliances, furniture and so on. It was, in fact, in Government shipyards that the first serious and really practical machines were made.

Samuel Bentham developed the rotary system of cutting as distinct from the reciprocating, and designed saws, planers, boring machines, tenoners and veneer-cutting machines. These were mostly patented between 1791 and 1793, but it would have been many years after that such machines became generally available to the woodworking industry generally. Marc Isambard Brunel also had much to do with early machines and had, in fact, patents on circular saws in 1805 and 1808. A bandsaw was patented by Newberry in 1808 but its success was hampered by poor quality saws, and it did not become really practicable until 1850 when reliable saws were made. Many planing machines were invented in the first fifty years of the nineteenth century, some in the U.S.A. Most early machines had wood frames. It was, in fact, not until the turn of the mid-century that all-metal frames were made.

The refined and somewhat delicate style as exemplified in Sheraton's works continued during the opening years of the century. The deterioration in his last designs, as shown in his *Encyclopedia,* 1804–07, mentioned in chapter 10, was little more than a pandering to a passing fashion, and it is fortunate that the more grotesque items were not made in greater numbers.

Other influences were at work, however, and to trace these we have to turn to France where the Consulate and Empire periods in which Napoleon was the dominant figure was producing a marked style known as Empire. This is dealt with more fully in chapter 12, but it had its counterpart here in a style sometimes known as English Empire. Its chief exponent was Thomas Hope, who published his *Household Furniture and*

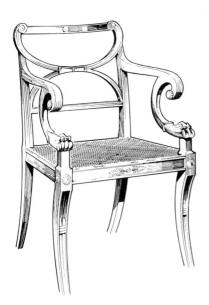

Fig. 1 Chair with sabre legs and caned seat. This is an extremely fine example of the chair maker's craft. Despite the somewhat complicated curvature of the back the construction follows conventional methods, the tops of the back legs being tenoned into the cresting rail and the moulded shaping worked across the joints. The curved rails fit together with a form of halved joint. The whole is in beech, and is black japanned with brass mounts. About 1810.

Fig. 2 Mahogany chair with brass inlay. This is of special interest in that the back legs are not set square with the front but line up with the slope of the side rails (see plan). This is a feature not found in chairs of earlier date. See also **Fig. 3F**. Owing to the pronounced side curvature this results in the bottoms of the legs converging. 1810–1815.

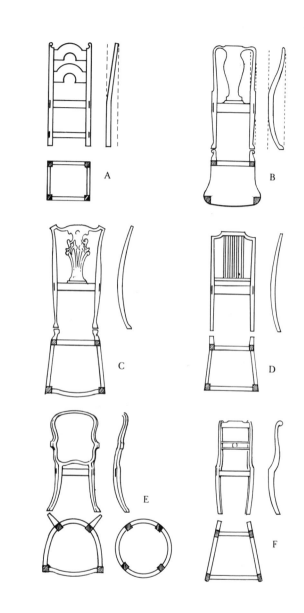

Fig. 3 How angle at which back legs are set in plan affects design. In examples **A** to **D** the back legs are square with the front; at **E** owing to the seat shaping they are mortised on opposite faces so that the legs diverge towards the bottom; at **F** the legs are in alignment with the sloping sides so that they converge. (See also pages 221–236).

Interior Decoration in 1807. This, like the French Empire, went back to Greek and Roman forms for its inspiration and produced some rather severe designs, mostly in mahogany with brass mounts in the form of vases, laurel wreaths, helmets, honeysuckle, lyres and so on. The style owed little to tradition, however, and although much of it was well made and of good proportions, it seems to strike a foreign and somewhat jarring note. Many of the shapes, especially chair and settee legs, seem curiously unsuitable for making in wood.

An attractive chair of about 1810 is that in Fig. 1, and shows a high degree of skill in its manufacture. The shaping of the members at the back, which necessarily have compound curvature owing to the plan curving combined with the elevation shaping, is beautifully worked out. The backward curve of the front legs is characteristic of the period and suggests Hope influence.

Another chair of about ten years later in date and of somewhat similar style is that in Fig. 2 and is given because it embodies a feature not found in chairs of earlier date. If any of the earlier chairs are examined, it will be seen that if a section is taken through the back legs at seat level the wood from which they are cut is invariably square with the front. Thus the chairs in Fig. 5, page 53 are as shown at Fig. 3A. Even when curved as in Fig. E, page 227 or Fig. I, page 231 they are still set squared as at Fig. 3B and C, any convergence at the feet being arranged by reducing the length of the seat rail and cutting the shoulders at an angle. Much the same applies to chairs in Fig. 2 and 3, page 160 and to that in Fig. 1. The only exception is in some Adam and Hepplewhite chairs, which have either round, oval, or hooped-shaped seats (see Fig. 4, page 146). In such chairs, owing to the shape, the rails are tenoned into *opposite* sides of the leg instead of into *adjacent* sides as in all other examples. As a consequence the back legs, owing to their backward curvature, are further apart at the bottom than at seat level. This is made clear at Fig. 3E.

Turning now to the chair under discussion, Fig. 2, note from the plan that the legs are not square with the front, but are parallel with the sloping sides as at Fig. 3F. As a result the legs are closer together at the feet than at the seat, this being produced without any *side* curvature in the leg. The shape looks more elaborate than it actually is, the shaping being confined to the side elevation of the back.

The chair in Fig. 4 dates from about 1850 and is more interesting than beautiful. The entire back is in papier mâché, this being compressed to shape and fixed to the back of the seat, probably with screws. There is in fact considerable dishing and shaping in the back and, when it is realized that it is no more than 12 mm.–15 mm. ($\frac{1}{2}$ in.–$\frac{5}{8}$ in.) thick in parts, it becomes obvious that such a back would be impracticable in wood. It is, in fact, an early example of a mass-produced chair and bears the marks of deterioration in design. As a matter of passing interest, note how the rails are tenoned into *opposite* sides of the back legs owing to the hooped shape, hence the divergence at the feet (see also Fig. 3E).

A couch showing the classical influence of Greece is that in Fig. 5. It

Fig. 4 Black japanned chair with inlay. The entire back is in papier mâché screwed to the lower framing. The back, legs, and seat rail are inlaid with mother of pearl. Mid. 19th century.

belongs to the Hope period of the early nineteenth century. Fig. 6 shows the rather heavy and stuffy appearance of a fully-upholstered couch in the middle of the century.

An interesting contrast in dining-tables made within about thirty to forty years of each other is shown in Fig. 7 and 8. The former, of the Regency period, has a certain grace and charm about it. Here again we see the old classical influence in the lyre motif. Light though it looks, the table is strongly built since the lyre-shaped pillar is not pierced right through, but is recessed at the surface only. The legs are dovetailed to the base. The whole top pivots, so that the table takes up little space when not in use.

In Fig. 8 we pass to a typical Victorian table of about 1850 which, whatever one may think of the design, is beautifully made. To us it may lack the refinement and grace of the earlier table, but it is an interesting speculation as to what folk of A.D. 2000 may think of it. For years it has been the practice of people to speak of Victorian furniture with something like contempt (though no one really familiar with it would ever deny its soundness of craftsmanship). Already, however, it is appearing in antique shops, especially early Victorian pieces, and it is quite on the cards that folk of the future will see beauty in what we now call heaviness and vulgarity. Fashions change, and nearly all generations are contemptuous of the works of their immediate forbears. Presumably the Victorian designers did not intentionally design things they knew to be ugly – and for that matter, who are we to talk in the second half of the twentieth century?

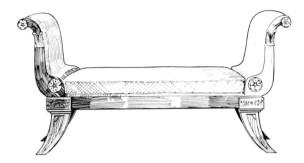

Fig. 5 Mahogany couch with upholstered seat and ends. The shaped legs and ends follow the style of Thomas Hope. The style is sometimes known as English Empire. Early 19th century.

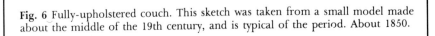

Fig. 6 Fully-upholstered couch. This sketch was taken from a small model made about the middle of the 19th century, and is typical of the period. About 1850.

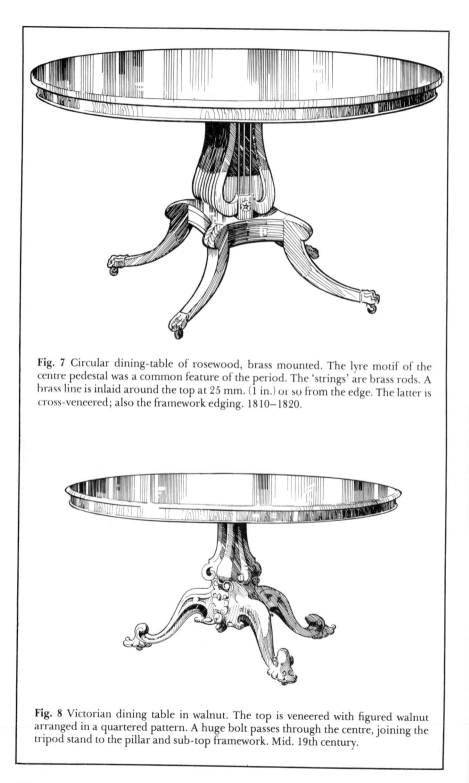

Fig. 7 Circular dining-table of rosewood, brass mounted. The lyre motif of the centre pedestal was a common feature of the period. The 'strings' are brass rods. A brass line is inlaid around the top at 25 mm. (1 in.) or so from the edge. The latter is cross-veneered; also the framework edging. 1810–1820.

Fig. 8 Victorian dining table in walnut. The top is veneered with figured walnut arranged in a quartered pattern. A huge bolt passes through the centre, joining the tripod stand to the pillar and sub-top framework. Mid. 19th century.

Fig. 9 Sofa table veneered with amboyna and marquetry. The flaps were invariably supported by brackets pivoted on knuckle or finger joints cut in wood. The legs were usually dovetailed to the base, and it was common practice to strengthen the joints with metal plates screwed to the underside. About 1815.

Fig. 10 Regency rosewood table with brass inlay. The table is one of a pair. About 1820. Photograph by courtesy of Foster of Putney, London.

Fig. 11 Variable size circular dining-table. The size can be increased by sliding out the triangular shaped pieces and inserting loose leaves. Mid. 19th century.

A type of table popular during the period under discussion was the sofa table, an example of which is given in Fig. 9. It was a type made popular by Sheraton and had hinged flaps at the ends supported by pivoted brackets. There were invariably drawers beneath the top. As the table was intended for use away from the wall the 'back' frequently had dummy drawer fronts. Its form during the Regency period is shown in Fig. 9, which shows the Greek influence of the period in the ornament. A similar type of table but having a folding top which, when opened, is swivelled round so that the lower framework supports it. Note the curious hump shape at the top of both Fig. 9 and 10. This was a typical feature of the period 1810 to 1830. An elaborate pedestal dining table of beautiful workmanship is that in Fig. 11.

The Regency version of the sideboard generally had cellaret pedestals reaching down to the floor and joined by a centre table portion quite open beneath. There was generally a drawer beneath the top as in Fig. 12. Tapered pedestals too were becoming popular, and the scrolled back shows the beginning of a feature which was often to assume quite gigantic proportions in the late Victorian period, and was often surmounted by an elaborate piece of carving, frequently of extremely fine crafsmanship. A sideboard of about 1870 is that in Fig. 13. The detail in it shows the arrival of the machine age.

Bedsteads in the late eighteenth century were generally of the four-poster type, but by the turn of the century two kinds developed. In the one the head-posts with abbreviated tester were retained and the foot-

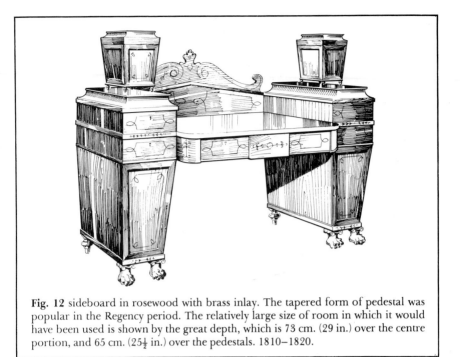

Fig. 12 sideboard in rosewood with brass inlay. The tapered form of pedestal was popular in the Regency period. The relatively large size of room in which it would have been used is shown by the great depth, which is 73 cm. (29 in.) over the centre portion, and 65 cm. (25½ in.) over the pedestals. 1810–1820.

posts eliminated. Frequently head curtains were used, and these could either be drawn right back or pulled a foot or so down the bed. The other type owed its origin to the Empire style of France. In this the bed was intended to stand with its side to the wall. There was a head and foot often sloped and having rather the appearance of a couch – the couch in Fig. 5 is in fact suggestive of the general form, though this is necessarily on a smaller scale. In some cases curtains were carried on to a shaped tester.

Perhaps the first impression one has of a mid- or late-Victorian room is one of overcrowded stuffiness. The drawing room mantelshelf would have its edge hung with deep drapery, and be covered with knick-knacks of all sorts; vases, framed pictures, brass ornaments, and so on probably grouped around a black marble clock or one with open movement, the whole contained within a domed glass cover. Above would be a large overmantel with centre mirror flanked with shelves and brackets, all holding their fancy ornaments. At each side of the chimney breast would be built-in cupboards about three feet high, and on these would be displayed stuffed birds beneath a glass domed cover and more knick-knacks. The furniture would consist of many upholstered chairs, including small easy chairs, Fig. 14, a single-ended couch, Fig. 15, with upholstered head and back and open foot, or later in the period a chesterfield with double ends and fully-upholstered. In the middle of the room might be an ottoman on which four people could sit all back to back. Against one wall would stand a tall upright piano with quilted silk

Fig. 13 Sideboard cabinet with decorated panels. About 1870.

Fig. 14 Small easy chair.

Fig. 15 Single-ended couch in walnut. About 1860.

Fig. 16 Tea poy in walnut. The inner containers are foil-lined and probably held two different kinds of tea. About 1845.

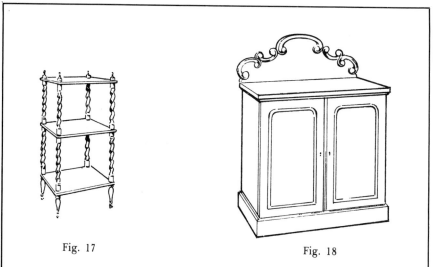

Fig. 17

Fig. 18

Fig. 17 Whatnot in walnut with twist legs. About 1850.

Fig. 18 Small chiffonier. Some examples were massive affairs with shaped front and marble top. About 1840.

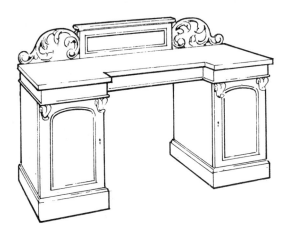

Fig. 19 Pedestal sideboard in mahogany. About 1840.

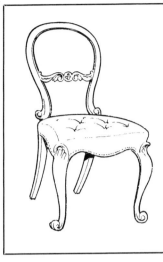

Fig. 20 Balloon-back chair. This chair had a buttoned seat and cabriole legs. About 1850.

front panel or fretted centre, and candle sconces at each side. A small table for the afternoon cup of tea, a backgammon table, possibly a tea poy (Fig. 16), and almost certainly that curious item the whatnot (Fig. 17) with its shelves to hold books, ornaments, etc. Another typical Victorian item was the davenport, a small writing desk with knee hole space, sometimes a sloping top, and with drawers on the side. Examples are given in Fig. 21 and 27.

The dining room would contain its large centre table which might be circular or, later, of the screw-extension type, which could be enlarged by turning a metal screw and inserting loose leaves. Incidentally some really fine work was put into these telescopic tables. In some cases the length increased from about 5 ft. (1·5 m.) to 14 ft. (4·2 m.), the whole working on grooved slides. In some tables there might be a separate centre leg that could be screwed in to support the middle, but quite often there were only the four corner legs. The trick was to make the slides slightly cambered in length. The manufacture of these tables appears to have been a specialized branch of cabinet making.

Along one wall would be a chiffonier, Fig. 18, or a great tomb-like sideboard, possibly veneered in mahogany, Fig. 19, or in solid oak with carving in either the free classical style or possibly pseudo-Gothic. Dining chairs from about 1840 onwards would probably be the balloon back type, Fig. 20. Chairs of the 1830 period and earlier usually had the top rail fitted above the uprights and projecting at the sides, but by about 1840 the tendency was for it to be rounded into the uprights in a continuous curve, Fig. 20. Another change that took place in chairs round about the middle of the century was the replacement of turned legs by the earlier cabriole style, usually with scrolled foot based on the French type.

In the bedroom would be a massive bed with half-tester and its complement of drapery and hangings, or from about 1870 onwards a

Fig. 21 Walnut davenport and balloonback chair. The davenport was used for writing. Mid. 19th century.

Fig. 22 Carved and inlaid chair designed for the Exhibition of 1851. An extremely fine example of the chairmaker's craft.

brass bedstead with head and foot of gate-like form with brass posts, rods, and finials. Humbler folk had a black iron bedstead. A dressing table with large mirror pivoted on shaped uprights would stand in front of the window, and there would be a wash-stand with marble top to hold basin and jug, and usually a high back partly to take splashes and also to support shelves. Fig. 23 shows a small separate mirror. The wardrobe in a large room might be a gigantic affair with cupboards and drawers. Cheaper commercial-grade wardrobes were quite light structures, Fig. 24, possibly painted. The small table in Fig. 28 might be used in either sitting room or bedroom.

The vast majority of houses were furnished with things that were the product of the commercial furniture factory in which basic machines had been installed. In general furniture was obtained from shops carrying a stock so that public choice was based on what manufacturers put on the market. This was in contrast with earlier practice in which furniture was made to order either from pattern books issued by cabinet makers or from designs prepared by designers or architects in consultation with the customer. The best work was undoubtedly of excellent craftsmanship, the machine being used to quicken processes, but still with much individual hand work and fine-quality timber. It seems, however, that the middle and late Victorian period was one in which advance in industry was the chief feature. Artistic appreciation showed some curious anomalies.

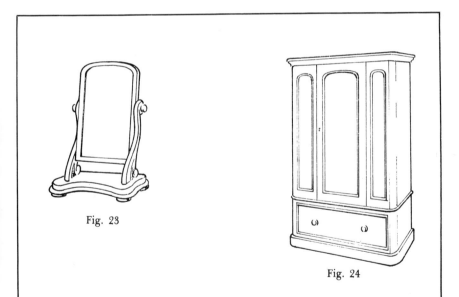

Fig. 23

Fig. 24

Fig. 23 Dressing table mirror of simple type. About 1860.

Fig. 24 Light wardrobe with rounded corners. About 1850.

Fig. 25 Jacobean style dining chair. About 1850. Photograph by courtesy of the Victoria & Albert Museum, London.

Fig. 26 Oak armchair designed by A. W. N. Pugin for Scarisbrick Hall, Lancs. A magnificent chair in the Gothic style. About 1840. Photograph by courtesy of the Victoria and Albert Museum, London.

Horse carriages, ships, locomotives, etc. were things of beauty, but houses and often the furniture in them seem to have declined from the high standard reached in the early nineteenth century and in the preceding century. In particular cheaper grades of furniture, largely the product of the machine, were turned out for an increasing market, things which had a sort of surface ostentation. It was a reaction against this that prompted such men as William Morris and Philip Webb to found their own businesses of designing not only houses but the entire contents for them, including tapestries, wallpaper, glassware, furniture, and plaster work. The designers struck an original note which owed much to the mediaeval Gothic period and nothing at all to the classical. The things they designed were on relatively simple lines, but were mostly designed to order and were consequently anything but cheap to make. They involved the use of much solid timber, and were frequently of vast size, and often with paintings by gifted artists.

It cannot be claimed that this work was anything but a drop in the ocean, the majority of people furnishing with items which were the product of the commercial factory. Taken generally the Victorian period was remarkable for the simultaneous popularity of several styles. Following the Greek type of which Thomas Hope had been the chief exponent early in the century, came Victorian versions of the Jacobean in which carved decoration and twist legs were the chief claim to Jacobean origin (see Fig. 25), the French with its flowing scrolls and shapes, and to a somewhat lesser extent the Gothic. The latter phase was popularized by Pugin, an architect who died in 1852, and authentic furniture designed by him is extremely fine. A splendid chair by him is shown in Fig. 26.

A point that strikes one about the general run of Victorian furniture is that it was invariably prodigal of timber. Easy chairs were frequently full of shapes, often compound, and must have cut into a lot of wood. Much the same applied to other items. Turned dining-table legs were often made from great 130 mm. (5 in.) squares, table tops were in solid Cuban mahogany or oak, and structural parts generally were of generous proportions. Veneers were saw-cut and relatively thick, in the production of which as much wood was lost in sawdust as was used in actual veneer. Prime timber was relatively cheap, the cost of felling and transporting to points of shipment by native labour being cheap; and indeed all labour costs whether in shipment or in the factory in this country were low compared with those of today. Furthermore prime timber was then plentiful. Inroads on timber forests were being made but there was still plenty of it ready for felling.

The finish of Victorian furniture was invariably French polish, and its application reached an extremely high standard. Even allowing for its drawbacks such as its liability to damage from spirit or water and its inability to resist heat, it undoubtedly had an excellent appearance and gave the effect, as it were, of being a burnished finish of the wood itself rather than looking like an outer transparent skin. Since it has now had about a century of patient polishing with wax, much of it in an age when

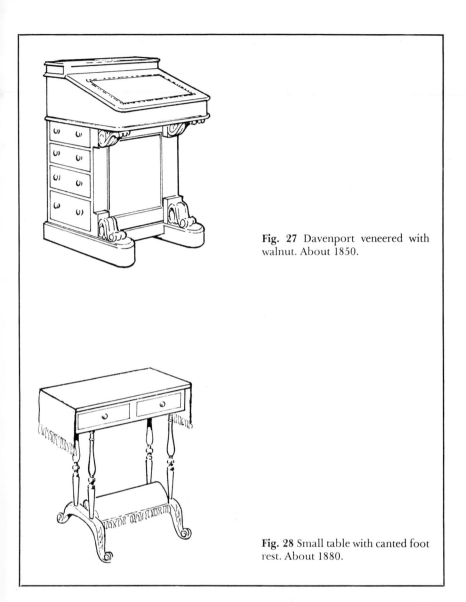

Fig. 27 Davenport veneered with walnut. About 1850.

Fig. 28 Small table with canted foot rest. About 1880.

there were many servants to do the work, it has acquired an excellent patina.

It is worth noting that in addition to the Victorianized versions of the Greek, Jacobean, French, and Gothic there were also some extremely fine reproductions of eighteenth-century furniture – Adam, Sheraton, and Hepplewhite – and in fact it is sometimes difficult to identify pieces, apparently belonging to the eighteenth century but made in Victorian times. Such work was invariably of extremely high standard. Perhaps the most remarkable is the satinwood cabinet made by Wright and Mansfield for the Paris Exhibition of 1867, now in the Victoria and Albert Museum, an exquisite piece of cabinet work.

Fig. 1 Cabinet with boulle marquetry. The work is carried out in brass and tortoiseshell, and is decorated with some particularly fine mounts of brass. The top is of marble. The accommodation consists of a centre cupboard with door and four drawers at each side. Louis XIV. Photograph by courtesy of the Victoria and Albert Museum, London.

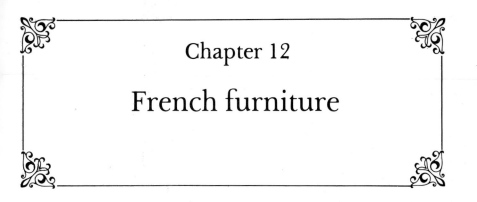

Chapter 12

French furniture

Louis XIV, 1643–1715

It is desirable for the person interested in English furniture to have at least a working knowledge of the French styles, if for no other reason than that of appreciating their influence on English work. To understand them thoroughly is a study equally as wide and intricate as that of English furniture (if not more so) and to do justice to the subject would call for a separate volume as large as the present one. In these few pages one can hope to do little more than point out the salient features.

Historically speaking the subject goes back farther than our own, for the continental craftsmen were far more advanced than the English, and have left more and better examples of their work to posterity. For the present purpose, however, the reigns of the three Louis, XIV, XV, and XVI are all that we are concerned with, for when speaking of French furniture it is the work produced during the period of these monarchs that one invariably calls to mind.

Louis XIV came to the throne in 1643, a time when the French Renaissance had lost much of its Italian origin and had developed a strong individual character. Whatever his merits or demerits as a king may have been, the world of art certainly owes much to him for the encouragement he gave to all arts and crafts. He was a man of most extravagant tastes and, living in a time when France was one of the strongest and wealthiest of European Powers, he was able to give full play to his fancies. His court was probably the most magnificent that Europe has ever known, and the daily extravagant ceremonial called for a setting for which nothing but the costliest and richest would do. Fortunately, this great impetus to fine work came at a time when men of considerable talent were seeking expression and it required only this talent on the one hand and the wealth and encouragement on the other to produce a style which, in its own particular way, has never been excelled.

Of the capable craftsmen whose names are outstanding probably the greatest was André Charles Boulle who was born in 1642 and died in 1732. He had experimented with a form of marquetry which had originated in Italy, and when the great tide of building and furnishing came he took it at its flood and developed this marquetry into a distinctive kind which for sheer exquisite workmanship, coupled with fine design, stands unique. It is often termed 'Buhl', and was carried out in brass or copper, and tortoiseshell, ebony and horn.

A brief explanation of how marquetry was produced was given in chapter 5. Two sheets of dissimilar materials were fixed together temporarily and the design cut through both with a fine saw. Two sheets were then separated and the parts interchanged so that in the one there would be a design of, say, brass on a background of tortoiseshell, and in the other the exact reverse. Thus it was possible to produce two cabinets of precisely the same outline and design, but the one the reverse of the other in the material of the design and background. The one was the 'counter' of the other, hence the terms 'Buhl' and 'counter'.

A typical Boulle cabinet is shown in Fig. 1, in which this rich marquetry work is an outstanding feature. In addition to the scrolling design of the inlay itself the whole of the brasswork is richly engraved, producing an effect which almost approaches the work of the jeweller rather than that of the cabinet maker. A point to note is that wood carving is almost entirely absent, the decorative effect, apart from the marquetry, being obtained entirely with rich brass mounts. Some of the leading artist-craftsmen of the time were engaged in the production of these mounts.

It was for the decoration and furnishing of the Palace of Versailles that the finest and richest work was produced, and the Palace, even as it stands today after the ravages of the Revolution, leaves one gasping at its sheer extravagant splendour. One has to remember that the furniture maker then was regarded as an artist and certainly the results seem to justify such a status. It is with something like a shock that one realizes that the cabinet in Fig. 1 was produced at the same time as the simple early walnut furniture in England. It is true that a colossal amount of money was spent on the production of such pieces, but it has to be admitted that the French cabinet makers were far in advance of our own. It is points like this that help one to realize why it was that a revolution of ideas took place when Charles II came to reign in England after years of exile spent in France.

The famous Gobelins factory for the production of tapestry was purchased by Louis XIV and cabinet-making workshops were established in it. Charles Le Brun became the director, and the world of art owes a great deal to his energetic leadership. Much of the finest work at Versailles was produced at the factory.

In general form the surfaces of cabinets were flat – at any rate early in the period. This is mentioned in particular because we shall see that in the next phase curved surfaces were introduced everywhere. The general decoration took the form of Boulle marquetry of brass or copper on a background of ebony or tortoiseshell, the design consisting of elaborate scroll work richly chased, allegorical figures, fruit and floral *motifs,* swags of husks and acanthus leafage, the whole in a somewhat free interpretation of the Renaissance. Bold ormolu mounts heavily gilded were fitted, these taking the form of lion masks, scrolled consoles, acanthus scrolls, human masks and deep nullings. Both straight and curved legs were used, the last named becoming more popular towards the end of the period in harmony with the tendency towards shaped work generally.

Louis XV, 1715–74

To appreciate the underlying causes of the changes in the type of furniture produced in Louis XV's reign it is necessary to know something of the historical events of the period. Louis XIV had died in 1715 when his heir was but five years old, and it became necessary to appoint a regent. The Duke of Orleans took the office, and he was virtually monarch until his death in 1723. There was thus a break in the extravagant court grandeur which was so essentially a feature of the reign of the late king. The wild expenditure of the seventy odd years of *le Grand Monarque,* too, had left its mark on the finances of the court and aristocracy. No country, no matter how powerful and prosperous, could continue for an unlimited time to spend money on pure aggrandisement to such an extent, and as a result there were but two alternatives: to live in a quieter way, or to find fresh sources of income. In the event a sort of compromise was effected. The aristocracy began to contract marriages with humbler but wealthy classes, bankers, merchants, and so on; and in place of the grandeur of the great salon so beloved by Louis XIV came the rise of the smaller boudoir. In fact the two periods are often referred to respectively as the periods of the salon and the boudoir.

Its effect on the furniture was that it was in its way equally rich, but was on a smaller scale. Then, too, the masculine grandeur gave way to an effeminate prettiness, a change quite in keeping with the general conduct of life. People began to look for elegance rather than grandeur, and to use ornament purely for its own sake.

We have had occasion to note in earlier chapters in this book that an idea, once it takes root, frequently is carried to extremes, and it thus happened that the tendency to introduce shaped work towards the end of Louis XIV's reign reached such a height in the succeeding reign that many cabinets were made with scarcely a straight line or a flat surface in them. This extraordinary use of curves is the keynote of Louis XV furniture. The skill shown in overcoming the difficulties that such work presented is amazing. One may or may not admire this flamboyant phase of French furniture, but no one can but admire the excellence of the workmanship. The fronts and sides of cabinets, bureaux, and so on were curved in both plan and elevation, and some idea of the difficulty of veneering over such a surface can be obtained by trying to lay a flat sheet of paper around a ball. Added to this was the fact that the whole was usually elaborately inlaid or given a decorative effect by the use of

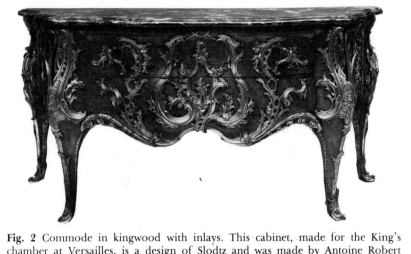

Fig. 2 Commode in kingwood with inlays. This cabinet, made for the King's chamber at Versailles, is a design of Slodtz and was made by Antoine Robert Gaudreau in 1738. The gilt bronze mounts were by Jacques Caffiere. Louis XV. Photograph courtesy of the Wallace Collection, London.

designs in which the varying direction of the grain of the wood was made to play a part.

So far as furniture was concerned the preference for gilded mounts in place of wood carving continued, and the workmanship of these was of an extremely high order. One may not care for the effect as a whole – it frequently appears restless and overdone, but regarded individually the work was extremely fine. The love of curves developed to an extraordinary extent, resulting in its fullness in what is known as the Rococo decoration. The term comes from two French words meaning rocks and shells, to which the ornament bears a certain resemblance. It is exemplified in Fig. 2 in which the elaborate scrolls and acanthus leafage can be seen. The chief exponents of the Rococo were Meissonier and Slodtz.

The French version of the cabriole leg reached its zenith during this period. It was essentially suited to the general and wide use of shapes. In a limited sense it bore a resemblance to the English version, but it had an entirely different spirit. The English leg at its best had a high, well-pronounced knee running abruptly into a square at the top, and terminating at the bottom with one or other varieties of the club or claw and ball foot. An example was given in Fig. 12, page 131. The French variety was of a more flowing shape. There was no square at the top, the shape either flowing naturally into shaped rails at the sides, or continuing with a concave curve upwards. At the bottom the foot was usually scrolled. The cabinet in Fig. 2 shows the typical French shape.

A great many varieties of woods were used; mahogany, amboyna, tulipwood, boxwood, rosewood, sycamore, ebony, and amaranth are amongst the commonest. Satinwood, too, was used towards the end of the reign, though this is more usually associated with the following reign of Louis XVI. Gilding and lacquering were popular. At first the lacquer work was imported from the East, or panels were prepared and sent to China to be lacquered, but later it was imitated in the French factories, though the detail in it was often faulty, western motifs being introduced in a somewhat incongruous manner. A firm of the name of Martin paid special attention to this lacquer work and produced a preparation known as Vernis-Martin towards the middle of the century. In its final stage this originally Oriental decoration became almost wholly westernized, the decorative artists painting allegorical subjects in natural settings on a lacquered background.

Towards the end of the reign a reaction against the elaborate Rococo work set in, and there came a revival of the classical spirit which was the keynote of the work in the following reign.

Louis XVI, 1774–93

The financial difficulties of the reign of Louis XV have already been noted. They still existed, in fact were increased, when the ill-starred Louis XVI came to the throne in 1774. The clouds were already gathering for the storm which was to break close on twenty years later. This, combined with the reaction against the Rococo work of the middle of the eighteenth century, produced a type of furniture in which the shaped work was largely, if not wholly, eliminated. Design became altogether more refined and returned again to the classical spirit, prompted largely by the excavations of Herculaneum which had been begun seriously in the middle of the century.

Then again the Queen of Louis XVI, Marie Antoinette, favoured simple country life; the elaboration of the preceding reign made no appeal to her and, although the movement towards simpler lines began before she was Queen, her influence undoubtedly encouraged the new feeling. It should be realized, however, that the term 'simple' is used relatively. Compared with the English, French cabinet work of Louis XVI was vastly more ornate. French furniture always was. It was just the natural national expression, but when it is compared with the full shaped work of the preceding reign the simpler and more refined feeling is apparent.

The chief characteristics of Louis XVI are the use of straight lines and flat surfaces with a delicate and refined treatment of the detail. Mouldings are small and the carving light and delicate. Gilded mounts are widely used (they were still largely preferred to wood carving) and the quality is of a very high order. The subjects take the form of rural, natural, and conventional objects; scythes, spades, lutes, pipes, birds, cupids, torches, ribbons, swags of husks, flowers, medallions, and acanthus scrolls. The last named are altogether less flamboyant than the ornament of Louis XV time. The woods used were the same as those of

Fig. 3 Table of the Louis XVI period. Marquetry of harewood and sycamore with gilt brass. Style of D. Roentgen. Photograph by courtesy of the Victoria & Albert Museum, London.

the previous reign with an increasing popularity for satinwood. Lacquer work was also still widely used, and was often bounded by gilded mouldings.

With the disappearance of the shaped work the cabriole leg lost much of its popularity, especially for cabinets and commodes, though it still was used for small bureaux and console tables in a lighter form. The light turned and square tapered leg was used largely, the last named often being recessed on its faces and decorated with gilded mounts fixed in the recessed panels. The chief designers were Riesener, Gouthiere and Roentgen.

All design is largely a matter of personal taste, but it is usually conceded that the work of Louis XVI shows French design and workmanship at its best. The furniture of Louis XIV had a certain grandeur tending to heaviness at its worst, this developing into an overdone elaboration in the following reign. In the last of the three reigns there was a reaction against the worst features, and the result shows a welcome restraint.

Readers wishing to study French furniture at first hand should examine the fine specimens at the Wallace collection, and the Jones bequest at the Victoria and Albert Museum, South Kensington. Those who are able to visit France should see the magnificent collection at the Palace of Versailles.

Empire

The period of the French Revolution during which Louis XVI and large numbers of the French aristocracy were executed was scarcely a time in which cabinet making could be expected to flourish. Wealthy people went into hiding or fled the country, and there was nobody left to order the fine quality and expensive furniture one usually associates with France of the second half of the eighteenth century. In fact, some of the famous ebenistes themselves were prosecuted for their close connection with the royalty and aristocracy. It was not until conditions had settled down under the forceful government of Napoleon that any revival of the making of fine furniture was possible.

It was then that was evolved the style which has become known as Empire. If Louis XIV furniture be characterized as solid magnificent grandeur, Louis XV as flamboyant elegance, all shapes and curves, Louis XVI as delicate refinement, sometimes verging on the effeminate, then the Empire can be reckoned as stately and dignified with a strong influence of the Greek, Roman, and Egyptian. Compared with the elegant style preceding it, Empire furniture is considerably more restrained, mostly with straight lines, usually in mahogany and invariably mounted with brass or gilt ornaments. These ornaments took the form of the Greek honeysuckle and vases, laurel wreaths, caryatid figures, martial helmets, torches, winged animals, and so on.

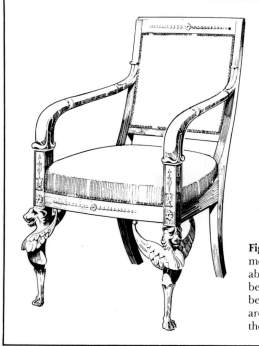

Fig. 4 Upholstered chair with brass mounts. The chair was made in about 1810. The wings of the beasts are in brass and are screwed beneath the seat rails. The feet too are brass, being socketed to fit over the stub legs. French Empire.

Presumably the style was a tribute to the leadership of Napoleon, the Emperor who had marched through Europe and beyond. It scarcely outlasted his final downfall in 1814, though its influence continued to be felt in this country during the Regency period.

Plates of measured drawings

The drawings on the following pages were made from old pieces of undoubted authenticity and their purpose is to provide the reader with details which could not possibly be shown in the perspective sketches given in the earlier part of this book. In most cases details of construction are given in addition to the purely decorative features, and the scales enable the sizes of the various parts to be approximated. The sections of mouldings, shapes of legs, carved details, handles, inlays and so on, are extremely useful to both those who, by comparing details and making deductions, wish to date a piece, and to the practical person who is making a reproduction.

The author would like to express his gratitude to those who have been kind enough to allow him to make drawings of pieces in their possession.

Readers who seek further examples of old pieces should see *Period Furniture Designs* by the same author. It contains over 40 measured drawings of period furniture with details of construction, many plates of details such as mouldings, and a series of full page plates showing the evolution of the various kinds of furniture.

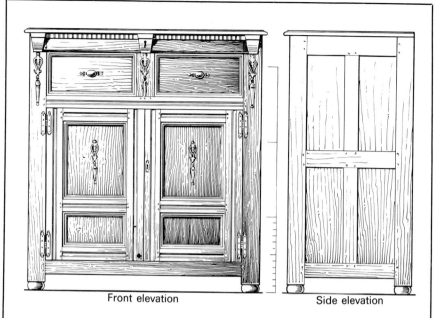

Front elevation   Side elevation

Jacobean cupboard. Drawn from a piece in the Geffrye Museum,
London. Mid. 17th century. A typical oak cupboard dating from the
middle of the 17th century. An interesting feature is that the upper
portion is really in the form of a chest, access to which is by means
of the hinged lid. The 'drawer fronts' are purely sham, consisting of
panels grooved into the main framework with a moulding around
the edges. The doors consist of grooved frames with an applied
moulding mitred around the inner edges. All rails and stiles are
channel moulded along the centre. The closing edges of both doors
are rebated so that they overlap each other.

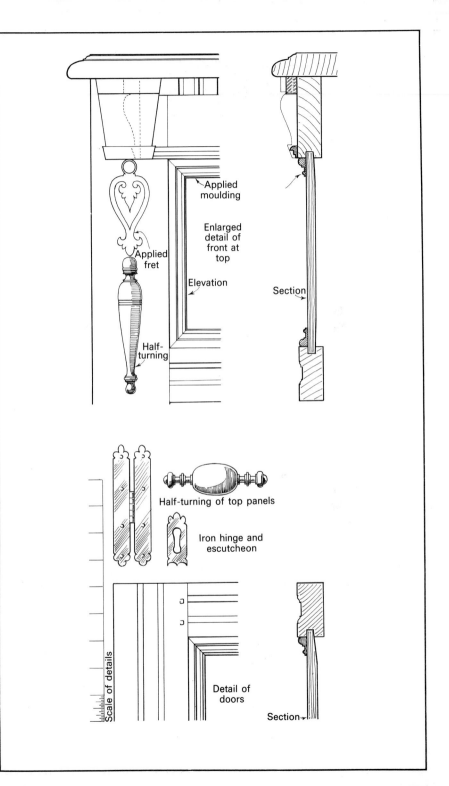

Applied
moulding

Enlarged
detail of
front at
top

Elevation

Section

Applied
fret

Half-
turning

Half-turning of top panels

Iron hinge and
escutcheon

Scale of details

Detail of
doors

Section

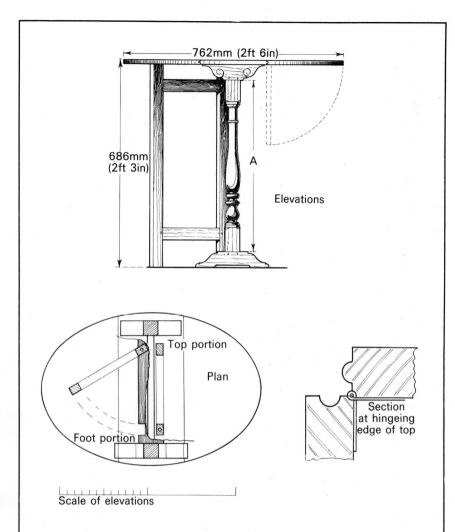

762mm (2ft 6in)

686mm
(2ft 3in)

A

Elevations

Top portion

Plan

Foot portion

Section
at hingeing
edge of top

Scale of elevations

Oak gate-leg table. This small table consists of a main framework with legs turned from 50 mm. (2 in.) squares. A centre rail joins them at the top whilst below is a rail lying flat. The gates are pivoted between this and the underside of the fixed top. The hingeing edges of the latter have a bead, and corresponding hollows are worked along the edges of the flaps so that there is no undue strain on the hinges when in the open position. In the top cross-pieces the scroll shape is continued by simple gouge cuts as shown. First half 17th century.

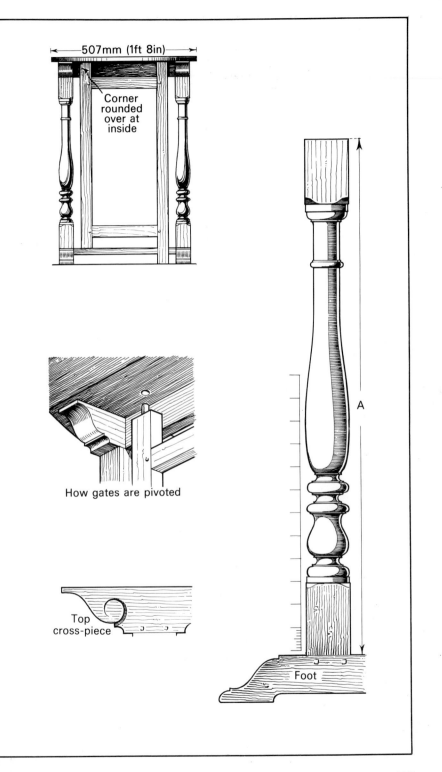

507mm (1ft 8in)

Corner rounded over at inside

How gates are pivoted

Top cross-piece

A

Foot

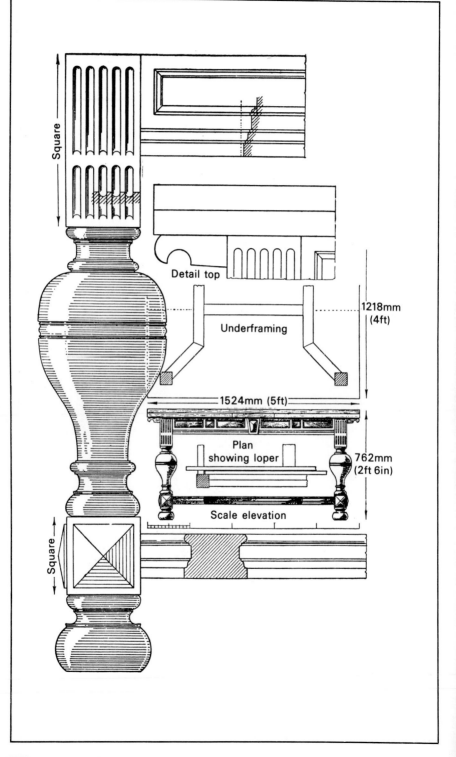

Square

Detail top

Underframing

1218mm
(4ft)

1524mm (5ft)

Plan
showing loper

762mm
(2ft 6in)

Scale elevation

Square

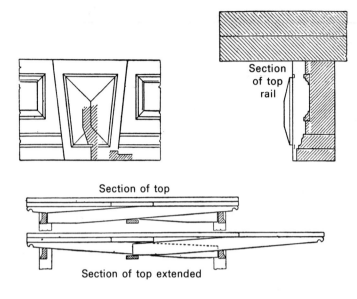

Section of top rail

Section of top

Section of top extended

Extending dining table. This is a well-proportioned oak table with 1524 mm. × 1218 mm. (5 ft. × 4 ft.) top, extending to 2744 mm. × 1218 mm. (9 ft. × 4 ft.). It shows considerable Dutch influence. The legs are 102 mm. × 102 mm. (4 in. × 4 in.) on the square, the bulbous turning being 152 mm. (6 in.) at its widest diameter. The square-edged tops are 28 mm. (1⅛ in.) thick, the rail under being 114 mm. (4½ in.) wide. The underframing rail, standing 108 mm. (4¼ in.) clear of the floor, has a section 75 mm. (3 in.) wide by 50 mm. (2 in.) thick. A sketch plan of the underframing is shown. The overhang of the top is 89 mm. (3½ in.) at each side so that the carcase size (over leg squares) is 1346 mm × 1041 mm. (4 ft. 5 in. × 3 ft. 5 in.). Drawn from a mid. 17th century piece.

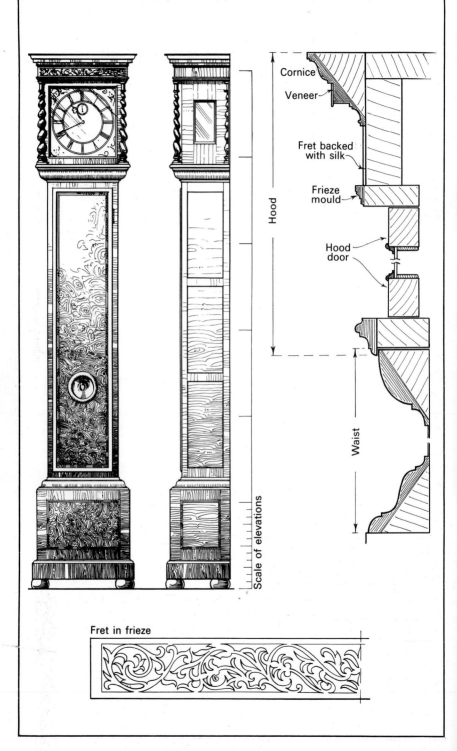

Cornice

Veneer

Fret backed
with silk

Frieze
mould

Hood
door

Hood

Waist

Scale of elevations

Fret in frieze

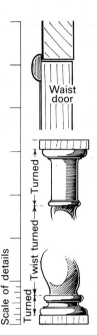

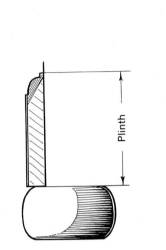

Waist
door

Turned → ← Twist turned → ← Turned

Scale of details

Plinth

Veneered walnut clock case of the Queen Anne period. Drawn from a piece in the Author's possession. This is typical of the kind of grandfather-clock case being produced during the last years of William and Mary's reign and the beginning of that of Anne. The flat top (later to develop into the shaped hooded type) with twist turnings opening with the door, and the rather long, narrow waist all point to the period. Another feature belonging essentially to the walnut period is the cross-grained mouldings and cross-banded panels with herring-bone detail.

The panels of the front are veneered with burr walnut, but the sides are of plain English walnut. In the waist the sides are panelled out with an inlaid black line. The movement is three-monthly, the pendulum beating once to the second, and the escapement is of the dead beat type. Early 18th century.

Mahogany bureau bookcase. This piece dates from about 1760 and is a typical example of the well-made, simpler furniture being produced in the Chippendale period. It is in dark Cuban mahogany with drawer linings of oak, and shelves of pine with mahogany facings.

An interesting feature is the method of construction used for the barred doors. Instead of an astragal moulding grooved over the bars (the method often used), the rounded member is entirely separate and is planted on the bar which is rebated out to hold the glass. Thus, instead of the door framing having a half-astragal worked around the inner edges, it is square with a rebate for the glass, and the half-round of the bars is planted on the face. The heading shapes of the pigeon-holes form the fronts of secret drawers.

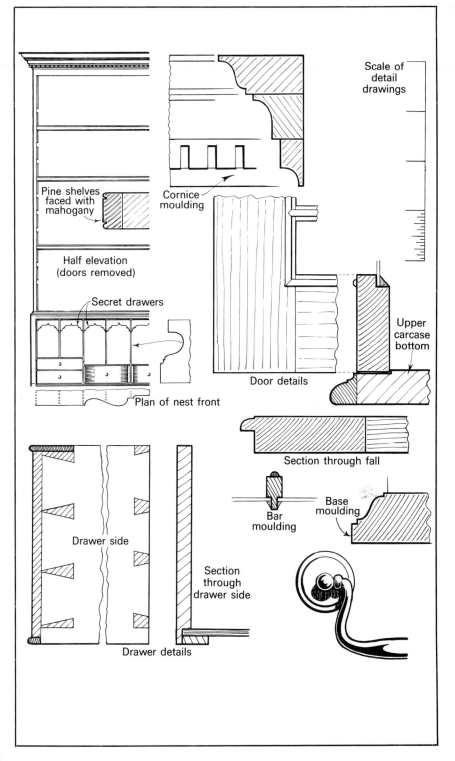

Scale of detail drawings

Pine shelves faced with mahogany

Cornice moulding

Half elevation (doors removed)

Secret drawers

Plan of nest front

Door details

Upper carcase bottom

Section through fall

Drawer side

Section through drawer side

Drawer details

Bar moulding

Base moulding

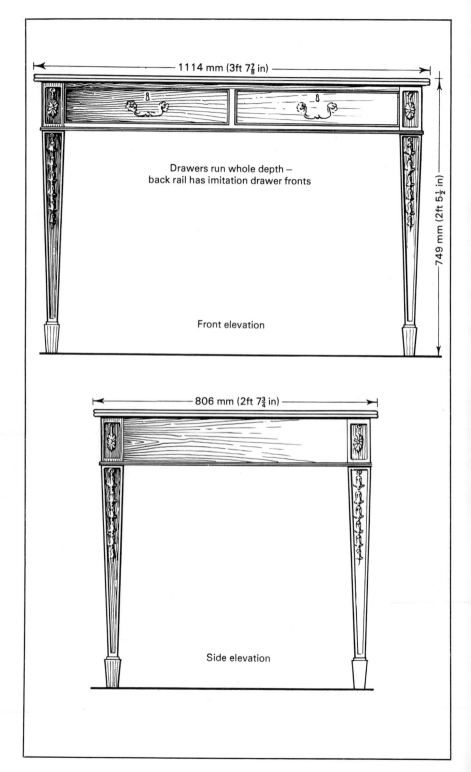

1114 mm (3ft 7⅞ in)

749 mm (2ft 5½ in)

Drawers run whole depth —
back rail has imitation drawer fronts

Front elevation

806 mm (2ft 7¾ in)

Side elevation

214

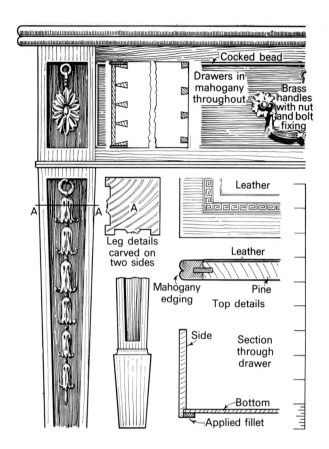

Cocked bead

Drawers in
mahogany
throughout

Brass
handles
with nut
and bolt
fixing

A —— A   A

Leg details
carved on
two sides

Leather

Leather

Mahogany
edging   Pine

Top details

Side   Section
through
drawer

Bottom

Applied fillet

Mahogany writing table of the Adam period. Made round about the
year 1770, this writing table follows closely the style of Robert
Adam, the architect who was designing furniture from about 1760
till his death in 1792. Typical features are the tapered legs and toes,
the delicate rendering of the carved husks in the recessed leg panels,
and the oval paterae at the top.

This piece was designed to stand in the centre of a room or in a
window recess, since the 'back' is as decorative as the front, the only
difference being that the drawer fronts are purely sham. The grain
of the bottoms runs from side to side, and they rest in rebates with
an applied fillet beneath to give a wider bearing surface. Drawn
from a piece in the possession of M. Harris & Sons, Oxford Street,
London.

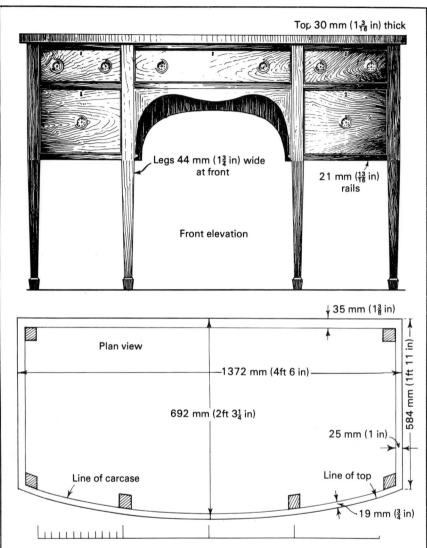

Top 30 mm ($1\frac{3}{16}$ in) thick

Legs 44 mm ($1\frac{3}{4}$ in) wide at front

21 mm ($\frac{13}{16}$ in) rails

Front elevation

35 mm ($1\frac{3}{8}$ in)

Plan view

1372 mm (4ft 6 in)

692 mm (2ft $3\frac{1}{4}$ in)

584 mm (1ft 11 in)

25 mm (1 in)

Line of carcase

Line of top

19 mm ($\frac{3}{4}$ in)

Mahogany bow-front sideboard. This represents a sideboard of about 1780. It is for the most part of mahogany veneered upon pine, with drawer linings of oak. In the earlier part of the 18th century a plain side table was used in the dining-room, this providing space for the various dishes for the table. Its lack of accommodation must have become increasingly obvious, however, and as a result separate pedestals were added during the second half of the century. The Adam sideboard, consisting of three separate pieces with the large urns surmounting the pedestals, is an example. Finally the pedestals were combined with the centre table, and the sideboard shown here is a development of this type. Late 18th century.

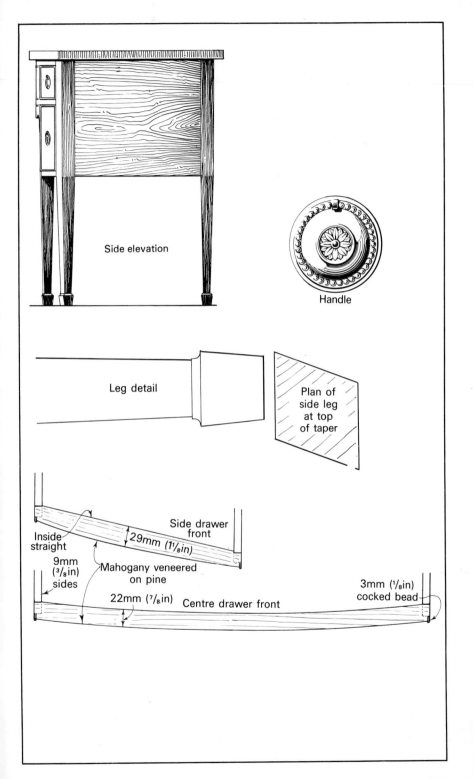

Side elevation

Handle

Leg detail

Plan of
side leg
at top
of taper

Side drawer
front

29mm (1⅛in)

Inside
straight

9mm
(³⁄₈in)
sides

Mahogany veneered
on pine

22mm (⁷⁄₈in)   Centre drawer front

3mm (⅛in)
cocked bead

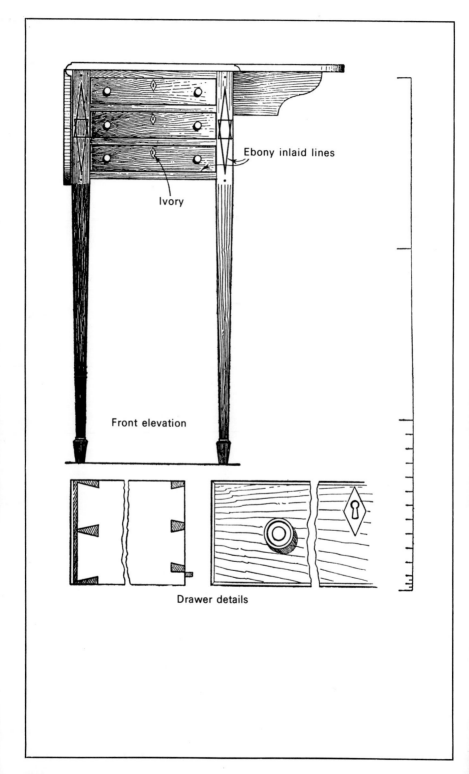

Ebony inlaid lines

Ivory

Front elevation

Drawer details

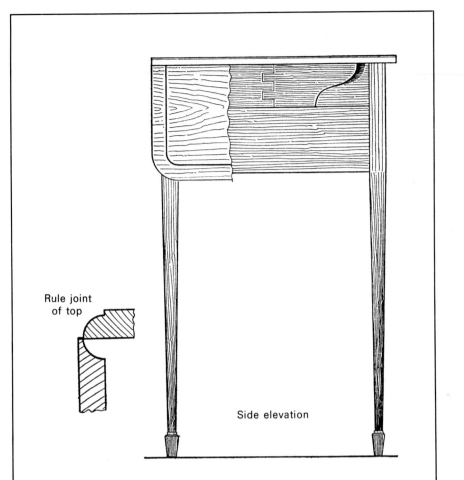

Rule joint
of top

Side elevation

Occasional table of the Sheraton period. This handy table is in
mahogany with inlaid lines of ebony and drawer linings of oak. At
the front there are two drawers only, the two lower fronts opening
as one. The back is treated similarly to the front but there are no
drawers, the 'fronts' being dummies. The top has two side flaps
connected with rule joints, and they are supported by finger jointed
brackets. About 1790.

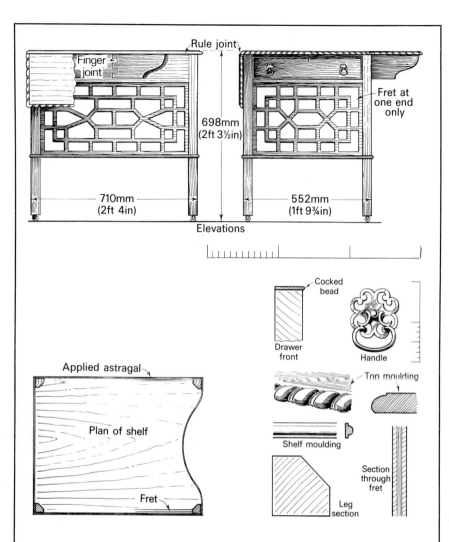

Rule joint

Finger joint

698mm
(2ft 3½in)

Fret at
one end
only

710mm
(2ft 4in)

552mm
(1ft 9¾in)

Elevations

Cocked
bead

Drawer
front

Handle

Applied astragal

Top moulding

Plan of shelf

Shelf moulding

Section
through
fret

Fret

Leg
section

Mahogany breakfast table. Dating from about 1760, this table belongs to the Chippendale style. The fixed top has two narrow flaps worked with the rule joint at the hingeing edges, and supported by brackets pivoted upon finger joints. The outer edges are nulled all round. An interesting feature of the lower frets is that they are made up of three thicknesses of 3 mm. (⅛ in.) mahogany glued together with the grain of the centre layer running at right-angles to those outside, similarly to modern plywood. It is thus considerably stronger than if it were made in solid wood. Drawn from a piece in the Victoria & Chelsea Museum, London.

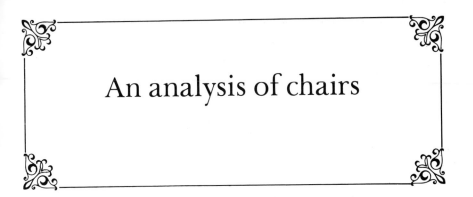

An analysis of chairs

At first thought there seems to be something obvious about the shape of a chair, considering that it has to conform to the human form. Yet its variations over the years have been little short of staggering. Wood as a material for chair making does impose certain restrictions. It is essentially stronger in its length than in its width, and one would imagine that the parts of a chair would therefore be straight, or have limited curvature only. In some cases this is true, but during the eighteenth century and later the most elaborate shapes were often used – ovals, shields, hoops, frequently with compound shaping. How did the chair maker overcome the problem?

In the most expensive chairs the designer no doubt prepared the design and left it to the practical chair maker to work out how it could be made and what timber it would require. Chair H is an example, being costly to make, partly in the timber it would cut into, and in the labour and skill involved. Those who combined practical ability with designing were often more cunning. An example is the chair, F, in which a most attractive compound shape has been produced within a limited section of timber. The fairly bold backward rake is inevitable, but the subtle curve of the elevation is contrived within a narrow width. The effect of this is heightened by the back seat rail shoulders being set at an angle so that the legs converge slightly towards the floor.

The convergence or divergence of the back legs towards the floor is an interesting point to consider. Sometimes it is definitely planned in the shape, but in other cases it is simply due to a practical reason.

In F the convergence of the back legs is obviously because of their having been set at an angle with sloping shoulders as already mentioned. It is due to an entirely different reason in J. Here the back legs are in alignment with the sloping side rails (see plan), so that, although the shoulders are square in elevation, the feet slope towards each other. In chair H the back legs spread outwards, not because of any shaping, but because the legs are contained *between* the curved seat rails (see plan). The same thing applies to any chair with seat which is circular or elliptical in plan.

From this it is obvious that convergence, divergence, or remaining parallel is not due to curvature (or only to a slight extent in some cases) but rather to the way the legs are set in relation to the rails.

Some chairs have compound curvature in the backs and are much more expensive to make than those with simple shaping, partly because more wood is needed in the former and because working costs are greater. Many Sheraton chairs had backs with only simple shapes as in example I. It is true that the back is thinned down above seat level, but only in a straight line. Other examples with simple curvature are A, B, C, J, and K (except for tapering).

Chair arms   Much the same holds good for chair arms as for backs, simple shapes being cheaper than compound curves (though the last named can be wonderfully effective). Examples are A, B (top plan), C, D, J, and K. In earlier work the front legs were continued upwards above the seat rails to form the supports A, B, C, D, but the tendency of the eighteenth century was to make the support a separate item set back from the front E, F, G, I. Toward the end of the century, however, there was a partial reversion to the old method, but the portion above the seat was invariably curved back as in H.

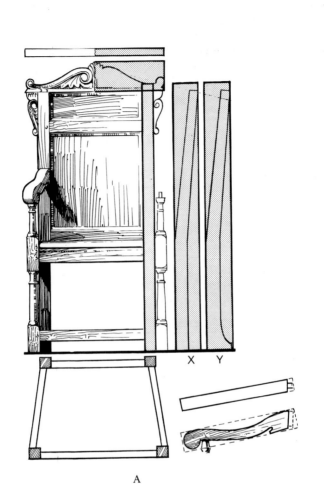

X   Y

A

Back is raked at the top X but is straight in front elevation. Sometimes the bottom was left thick Y to lessen any tendency to tilt back. In both cases the shaping is of the simplest type and occurs in side elevation only. Top rail is also flat. Front leg is continued up to support arm. First half 17th century.

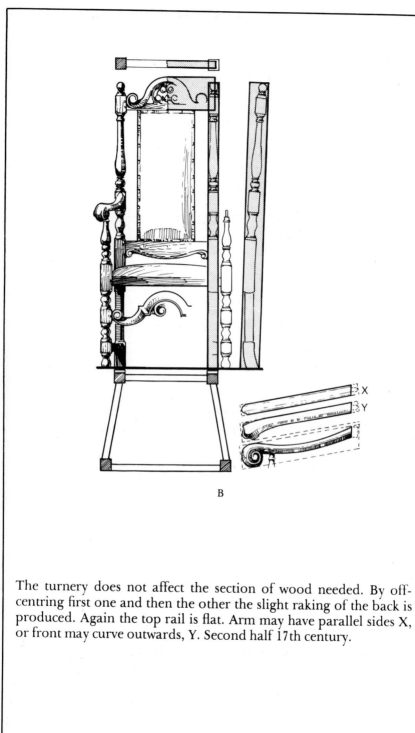

B

The turnery does not affect the section of wood needed. By off-
centring first one and then the other the slight raking of the back is
produced. Again the top rail is flat. Arm may have parallel sides X,
or front may curve outwards, Y. Second half 17th century.

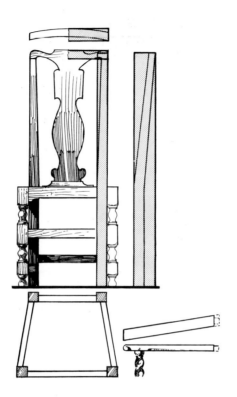

C

This is of special interest in that, although the extra thickness of wood is needed in the side elevation only, the maker has endeavoured to create the illusion that the front also is shaped by tapering the back uprights towards the top and shaping the top rail in an acute curve to meet them. In reality there is no front shaping at all. On the other hand the top rail has a slight backward curve. Late 17th century.

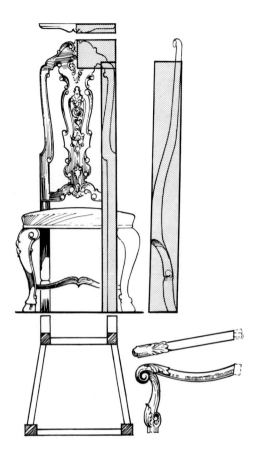

D

Here the maker has made his first adventure into compound shaping, and it is obvious that the cost is considerably greater, partly because of the extra wood needed, but also owing to the cost of working the shape in both front and side elevation. Curiously, however, the top rail has reverted to the flat. Arm of period given below. Early 18th century.

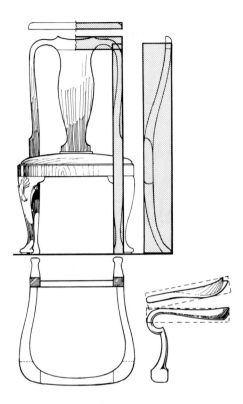

E

The trick of compound shaping having been discovered, it was developed. In this example, however, there is an economy in that the uprights are cut from a section no thicker than is needed for the squares at seat level (front elevation). Some Queen Anne chairs had much more elaborate front shaping and needed more wood accordingly. In this chair again the top rail is flat, though many chairs of the period curved backwards. About 1715.

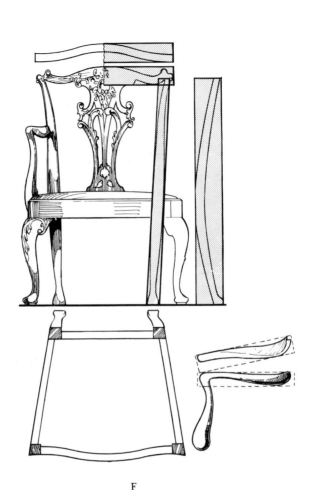

F

Here we have compound shaping yet with a certain economy, particularly in the front elevation. It is interesting to note that the delicate curve is contained within the total width of wood at seat level, so that no extra section of wood is needed, a delightful example of evolving a shape within the limits imposed by the material. The effect is enhanced by inclining the legs toward the floor. About 1755.

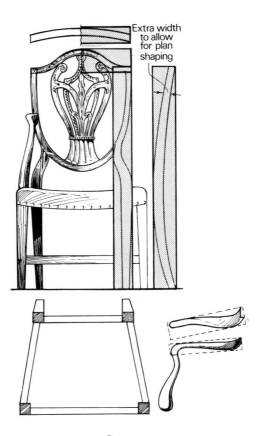

Extra width to allow for plan shaping

G

There is considerably less restraint in this model, both front and side elevation calling for considerably greater section of wood than at seat level. It is consequently an expensive chair to make. Since the top rail bows backwards extra wood is needed here, and the back uprights need to be cut out extra wide to allow for the plan shaping. About 1775.

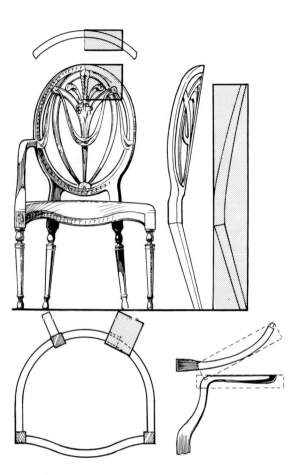

H

An extremely costly chair to make. There is obviously compound shaping, and an extra complication is that in plan the seat is D shaped. This means that the plan shaping of the back is extremely pronounced. Furthermore, a side elevation does not reveal the true shape because the back legs are contained between the ends of the rails (see plan). Incidentally, one result of this is that the legs splay outwards instead of going straight back or converging slightly. About 1775.

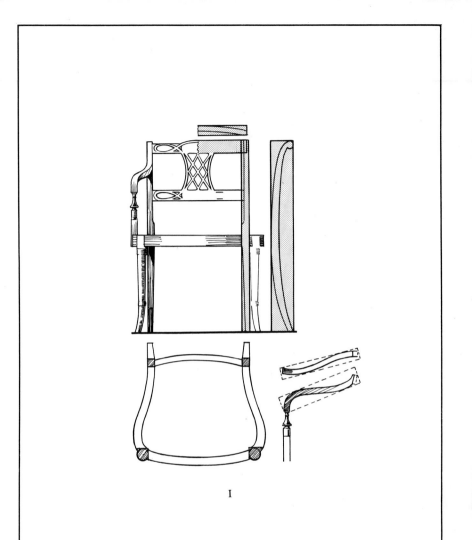

I

Although quite an expensive chair to make there is a marked return to economy since there is no shaping in front elevation, just a thinning down above seat level. This was a feature of many Sheraton chairs. The back rail has limited curvature only. About 1800.

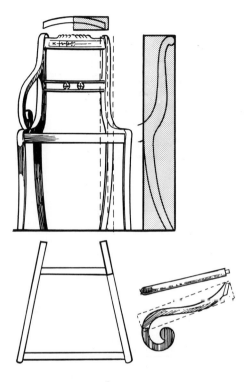

J

This chair has no compound shaping, although the side curvature is very pronounced. The legs converge towards the bottom, but this is not because the rail shoulders are at an angle in elevation but because the legs are in alignment with the side rails (see plan). About 1815.

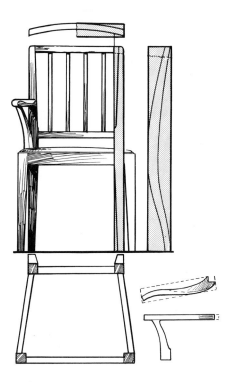

K

A chair that has much in it that is traditional. There is no compound shaping, but the back uprights are thinned towards the top, and the legs tapered from below the seat rails. Few modern chairs have compound shaping, largely owing to the cost. Present day.

Front legs To a large extent the shape of a leg affects the section needed to work it, but not always entirely so. For plain turned legs the size is obvious – in fact the usual plan was to start off with a square of fixed size and arrange the turning to come within it. Much the same applies to square tapered legs. On the other hand it was common practice to build up squares locally to enable a larger shape to be worked, especially on parts not subjected to strain. Thus bulbous legs often consisted of a main centre square of the minimum section required, with applied pieces glued on at the fullness to enable the shape to be worked. Then again cabriole legs invariably had ear pieces glued on locally to avoid the necessity for so large a section of wood, quite apart from the work involved.

In the case of armchairs it was the invariable practice in early oak chairs to carry the leg above the seat to form a support as in A and B, pages 223 and 224. Later it became fashionable to make the arm supports separate and set them back from the front F and G, pages 228 and 229. Later again there was an occasional reversion to the original idea, especially in the late eighteenth century as at H, page 230, though the support was frequently swept back in a curve. Practically the only type of front leg having compound curvature is the cabriole G, H, I, J, O, and the foot of E, pages 235 and 236. That at D appears to be compound, but in fact it is only a flat-cut leg set at 45 degrees. The carving of course elaborates the shaping. At F the shape is plain turned, and the scrolls carved into the bulbous portion.

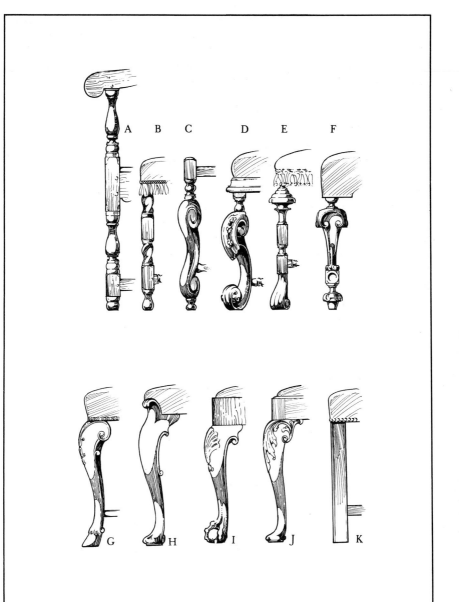

A Oak. About 1600; **B** Walnut. Mid. 17th century; **C** Walnut. About 1675; **D** Beech. About 1690; **E** Walnut. About 1690; **F** Walnut. About 1690; **G** Walnut. Early 18th century; **H** Walnut. About 1715; **I** Walnut. About 1720; **J** Mahogany. About 1755; **K** Mahogany. About 1760.

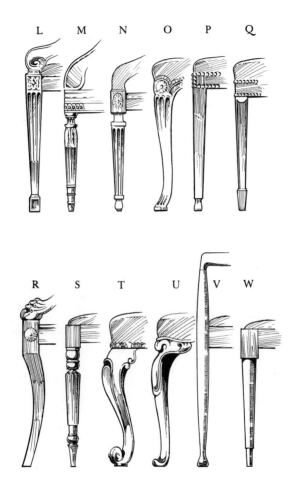

L Mahogany. About 1770; M Gilt. About 1777; N Mahogany. About 1775; O Mahogany. About 1775; P Mahogany. About 1775; Q Mahogany. 1783; R Beech. About 1810; S Beech. About 1820; T Walnut. Victorian; U Mahogany. L'art nouveau; V Beech. Present day. W Teak. Present day.

Index